OVERCOMING

BETRAYAL

OVERCOMING

BETRAYAL

Ron DePriest

DESTINY IMAGE® PUBLISHERS, INC.
P.O. Box 310, Shippensburg, PA 17257-0310

*"Speaking to the Purposes of God for this Generation
and for the Generations to Come."*

This book and all other Destiny Image, Revival Press, Mercy Place, Fresh Bread, Destiny Image Fiction, and Treasure House books are available at Christian bookstores and distributors worldwide.

For a U.S. bookstore nearest you, call 1-800-722-6774.
For more information on foreign distributors, call 717-532-3040.
Or reach us on the Internet: www.destinyimage.com

ISBN 10: 0-7684-2402-X
ISBN 13: 978-0-7684-2402-7

For Worldwide Distribution, Printed in the U.S.A.
1 2 3 4 5 6 7 8 9 10 11 / 09 08 07 06

DEDICATION

As you read this book you will hear the cry of my heart and the longing of my soul. You will realize that you are not alone, for like you, betrayal has also deeply affected my life and the lives of those who have been close to me.

There are two individuals who have walked this journey with me. They have always been there for me and today they are beneficiaries of all God has brought us through. My daughter, Ronda, who has prayed and believed that her daddy was a person who could change; and her mother, Minnie, my lady, who will not stop believing in me and for me.

Mostly this book is dedicated to our grandchildren. When I look at them, I see the next generation of believers who will walk in His presence with more understanding, more simplicity, more purity, and more devotion to the one true God. What I do today is to help their tomorrow.

ACKNOWLEDGEMENTS

It is difficult to recognize all those who have helped us through times of joy and times of struggle—we have been blessed by so many. From the beginning of my walk with God until now, there are those who have loved me and those who have believed that I was guilty and should quit. I say thank you to them all. I know that the struggles in my life have allowed me to triumph over satan and the seeds of betrayal. This book is a result of those triumphs and discovering the differences between God's nature and my own.

I also want to thank Patty Ash for her heart to see that this book was completed in the manner that you see. She has taken her God-given ability to help and used it for His glory. David and Patty Ash are true friends.

ENDORSEMENTS

Occasionally a book comes along that reaches across denom-
inational lines, crosses gender lines, and even crosses cultural
and racial lines. Ron DePriest has written such a book! *Overcoming
Betrayal* provides a path with practical steps to walk out of the
web of betrayal. Ron openly shares his struggle for freedom. He
also highlights biblical characters who dealt with betrayal. He
powerfully points the reader away from natural man's responses to the struggle. Ron then leads his audience toward be-
holding the glory that results from obedience as they stay the
course in their pursuit of God. I highly recommend this book to
all who desire to be free from the enemy's trap called *betrayal*!

Barbara Wentroble
Founder, International Breakthrough Ministries
Author, *Prophetic Intercession; Praying With Authority;
You Are Anointed; Rise to Your Destiny, Woman of God*

Few Christian leaders have dared to approach the subject of betrayal head-on. Ron DePriest, however, is one who has accepted the challenge. In this fascinating book he exposes his own near-death experience with betrayal; then step-by-step he shows us how to recognize it, avoid it, deal with it, and overcome it. This book carries a powerful message for all of us!

C. Peter Wagner, Presiding Apostle
International Coalition of Apostles

Dr. DePriest's book is a must read for the Body of Christ. At one time or another, all of us have been betrayed and have struggled with the damaging effects of betrayal. This book exposes the root of betrayal and the subtle tricks the enemy uses to ensnare mankind and gives practical application for recovering from the bondage of the past.

If you have come to what seems to be a holding pattern in your life, *Overcoming Betrayal*, will provide help to break free from this vicious cycle that has kept so many from fulfilling their destiny.

Drs. David and Vernette Rosier
Pastors, Panama City Fellowship Church of Praise, Inc.

Apostle Ron DePriest has written this timely book so that every Christian may overcome the wounds of betrayal. This refreshing revelation teaches believers to live free and follow Jesus, fulfilling their destiny by the grace of God and the power of the Holy Spirit.

Pastor Joseph Dugas
Crossroads Ministry Centre

Sometimes an author will write a book based upon a personal revelation and others will write a book based upon their experiences. Unfortunately, not enough authors write books that are influenced by revelation *and* experience. This is one of those books. Ron DePriest has the revelation and the experience to qualify him to write on the subject of overcoming betrayal.

Overcoming Betrayal is a timely book for this generation. There are few who have never experienced the bruise of betrayal. I don't know if there is any pain worse than the soul-stinging power of being betrayed by those we love and trust. It is my prayer that this book will find its way to all those who are suffering its deadly sting.

Ron's words are more than theory. They are written with the pen of his own blood and tears. His words take you above his own grief as he offers a pathway to healing. *Overcoming Betrayal* is the medicine you need to cure the broken heart of deceit and disloyalty.

Don Milam
Vice President, Destiny Image Publishers
Author, *The Ancient Language of Eden*

Ron DePriest, through the pain of rejection and betrayal, has received a revelation from the Father that is so important today. I heard a quote once, "uncertainty is the curse of authority." Betrayal causes us to lose our identity; and thereby we become uncertain about who we are in Christ. We lose our God-given authority over satan and his lies.

Chapter 12 is a must-read by everyone who opens this book. It is a revelation, a tool, a weapon to defeat every enemy lie of satan.

Great book, Ron! I'm always amazed how God loves some people so much that He knows He can share with them pain because He knows they will turn it around for His glory, like Job. Thanks!

Bishop Bart Pierce
Rock City Church, Baltimore, Maryland

In his cutting-edge book on betrayal, Ron DePriest divides between soul and spirit. Without a doubt, it is the most insightful material that I have read on the subject. This book is revelatory in defining what betrayal is; where it comes from; its damaging, lingering effects; and, most importantly, how in a superb Christlike fashion to effectively deal with it and be healed from it by the power of God. According to Matthew 24:10, betrayal is a key last days' issue that we will have to overcome. Ron DePriest is one of those who in his years of ministry has walked through the fires of betrayal and has accessed a grace that has made him better rather than bitter.

Pastor Les Bowling
Eagle Rock Ministries

TABLE OF CONTENTS

FOREWORD

Here is a book and an experience I know many will relate to—betrayal! Many of us have experienced the painful tragedy of betrayal. Just reading the title may bring up an experience you are still dealing with. Do not let the emotion keep you from reading this book!

Betrayal is one of satan's greatest weapons to destroy your life, the life of a leader, and relationships with those you love. It is set against your success, achievement, and destiny. I have experienced the emotion of the death of loved ones, yet the pain of betrayal by those close to me has been the worst. I believe it is truly part of a diabolical plan to destroy your life success. It causes many never to trust again. They say, "You can't trust _____" (you fill in the name) or "I hate all _____" (you fill in the blank).

Leaders, or anyone God plans to use in a mighty way, are particular targets of betrayers. Jesus was betrayed by Judas, Peter, and others who deserted Him in His hour of need. Joseph was betrayed by all of his brothers; Moses was betrayed by Korah and his brother and sister. Elisha was betrayed by Gehazi, David by his son Absalom, and the list goes on and on. Betrayers are people who have become close to you. They are those who are trusted, someone you may have great hope for, poured much time into, cared for, loved, parented, or married. Yet there is a way to overcome!

Here is a book written by a man who has been there, survived, and learned the valuable overcoming lessons. Ron DePriest has won the victory over betrayal. I believe you or someone you know can also win the victory! Read on and get the insight you need for a breakthrough to overcome and get back on the road to success! Turn the page and get your victory!

Apostle John P. Kelly
President/Founder, LEAD
(Leadership Education for Apostolic Development)

INTRODUCTION

There are few actions or emotions that penetrate deeper into the very core of our existence than betrayal. Regardless of class, economic stature, job description, or culture, all people have felt betrayed at least once in their lives. Betrayal can come from many different venues: close relationships, business partnerships, work experiences, ministry connections, even the actions taken by government or agencies that some may look to for support.

Whether betrayal is real or only perceived, it has the same damaging aftershock. Betrayal is the root of various damaging emotions that can ultimately lead to corrosion in our lives. Anger, bitterness, rejection, and isolation are only a few of the emotions betrayal leaves behind. Perhaps the most dangerous result of betrayal is the high propensity for betrayal to reproduce itself in the life of the one betrayed—making it almost unstoppable.

Although betrayal can be a great destroyer, many times it is the silent stealing away of identity that overtakes an individual and sends them spiraling into a search for value and worth. Trust can be shaken and confidence laid to ruin in the wake of betrayal.

The great news is that the effects of betrayal can be shifted from a negative force in your life to a positive, life-affirming transformation. This is possible when we realize that any challenge or obstacle can be used to reveal more of our internal character. The stronger our character becomes, the more we are able to face and successfully overcome the trials of life.

Betrayal specifically identifies the source of our trust. It is only when our lives are grounded on a solid foundation that we can ever begin to truly open up our lives and begin to become contributors to mankind rather than takers only. After we are free to trust again, we will begin to seek out the heart of the Father to find identity. In that identity, we find purpose and are empowered to fulfill our destiny. Only then can we reach beyond ourselves to help others.

You are not alone. As you walk through the pages of my personal journey of becoming vulnerable enough to truly stand strong in the face of deep betrayals, I pray that you will face your own betrayals—past or present—and find healing. Whether you have been stripped of everything as I was, or just wounded right below the surface, you need to be healed. There is a place of acceptance, approval, identity, and authority where you can recognize and remove the effects of betrayal in your life—it is in the presence of the Father.

Chapter 1

TORN HEART

Books have been written on just about every subject known to man. Still, there is one subject that touches every life that cannot be dealt with by using snappy acronyms or "7 Steps to Healing." It is the subject of the torn hearts, shattered trust, and broken lives caused by betrayal. This is not a light-hearted topic with well-placed laughter cues and warm-hearted fuzzy moments, but it is a topic we must understand. Betrayal causes hurt resulting in an abundance of tears. This book will help you realize that the love of Christ can transform tears of pain into refreshing streams.

Betrayal can be experienced on various levels through loved ones who are intimately close, ministry relationships we have trusted, and even work-related situations that have burned us. Throughout 30 years of ministry I have seen betrayal between husbands and wives, parents and children, employers and employees, and church congregations. Almost everyone can recall a personal account of betrayal. My account is about the betrayal I experienced but it is not my story alone. Betrayal affects everyone who is connected to you—families, friends, and followers. One betrayal is powerful enough to spread hurt and pain through a multitude—it is never about just one person. In fact, this account of betrayal affected over 200 families.

TORN APART

Things were going great. My wife, Minnie, and I had a church with more than 200 members. The people were strong in faith and moving toward taking the city. We had started churches in other states and they, too, were growing strong. I was spending time in these churches speaking to men of God and their congregations. We were surrounded by a network of wonderful people looking for ways to actively serve God. In the mix of ministering, we had also started a small business that seemed to be going well.

In the middle of this season, I received a visit from a church elder. He had served our church faithfully and my heart was to serve and help him. He told me that he was in debt and could not pay his bills. Beyond informing me of his financial trouble, he seemed to expect the church to pay for his personal money management dilemma. This elder held a paid position at the church, and his salary was almost the same as mine. Because there was no previous indication about financial trouble or lack, his situation caught me completely off guard. After much discussion, I wrote a check using church funds to cover his bills.

The man took the check and as he reached my office door, I told him that because he had not sought counsel or help before the situation became so serious, he should not have demanded that the church or I cover his bills. I firmly told him not to allow this type of circumstance again or he would be disqualified as an elder; he would be removed from serving and his family would be asked to leave the church. The elder drove directly to my spiritual leader and accused me of not loving or caring about him. The man who watched for my soul took the accusation without witnesses and I didn't know about their meeting until much later.

A few weeks after my meeting with the elder, something out of the blue happened which became the catalyst for change that would turn my entire life inside out and upside down. During a routine business meeting, my appendix burst. The effect was so severe that doctors expected me to die. I was placed in the critical care unit and many doubted whether I would leave the hospital alive. In fact, many people died while in that unit so when the news of my release came to the nursing staff, they shouted down the hallway, "Room 12 is going home!" God's miraculous power intervened and days later I was sitting in my own living room, still very weak as I began the slow recovery process. During a follow-up visit, they wanted to put me back into the hospital but I refused because I didn't have medical insurance. Consequently, I was prescribed strong medication in an effort to fight off the infection that filled my body.

It was while I was in this condition that I received a visit in my home from the man I looked to for guidance. He told me that the elders were angry and that we needed to have a meeting. I was accused of being without gentleness or compassion—my actions were too hard, too strong, and too mean. I was told that I required too much from the people. The accusations progressed into a full, all-out assault on my character. I asked his advice about what to do. He told me the best thing would be to step down and let him take over the church and the network for a little while.

Following his counsel, I met with him and the elders and handed over the keys to everything. The elders were eager to step in—they were all too happy to take charge of a strong church full of great people. The man who covered me spiritually promised I would be taken care of during this time—within 30 days I was completely broken, and so was every promise the man had made.

I stepped down from the church and out of the network. The action "step down" seems simple and yet it was really too complicated to grasp. I had started this church from nothing, in our own home. People who had heard me minister across the country had moved their lives and families to our location to be a part of the work. God was revealing people's gifts and restoring families. Men had come to the training center to study the practical application of walking with God. We were all learning and growing together. It was an exciting time as God was moving and changing lives.

Minnie and I had put our heart into every individual in the church, falling in love with them as if they were our own flesh and blood. We had enjoyed countless hours of working and playing together, building up families and sharing tears of sorrow as loved ones passed on, as well as screams of excitement as prayers were answered and dreams fulfilled. We had given beyond the point of sacrifice to house members of the church, to support them financially, emotionally, and spiritually. We had broken bread with these families, shared in their most intimate moments. Our hearts had been entwined with their lives and to step down meant to rip away the soft, pliable tissue of our hearts leaving only a jagged edge of sharp pain. This was a special group of people—we were undone with love for them. Their destiny, their lives meant so much to me that the thought of any hurt coming to them was worse than the thought of personal death.

This love drove me to accept the instruction of the man who watched for my soul. So, I stepped down even when it went against the very foundational conviction of my soul. I believed the people would be able to overcome any situation placed before them. After all, it was only to be for a short season.

Acting in a state of complete trust and belief in only the best intentions of the men around me, I delivered a message to the church about not allowing bitterness to enter into your heart. At the end of the message I told the church that the elders would be in charge while I took time off to rest and recover. Some of the people were shocked while others knew exactly what was happening.

THE FINAL NAIL

Behind the scenes, one man was leading a revolt to completely push me out of the picture. Meetings were held without my knowledge and plans were made for me to leave and start over in a different city. The church would be taken over because the elders believed that the people did not want me there. The people were told to stay away from me completely—for reasons I still do not understand.

A strong love for the people mixed with the emotional trauma of the hospital visit and the physical toll of prescription medications clouded my judgment and resolve. I gave in to advice given by a Trojan horse. The one man in whom I had trusted and had pulled close to myself revealed a heart of betrayal, and a plan to overthrow the ministry foundation I had built in order to build his own kingdom and practice his personal agenda.

What started as one elder taking over the church congregation became an initiative to take over everything. With a vengeance, he came after the building, financial contributions, Minnie's car, my own personal sound system, and countless other material things. Everything was taken from us except my home and a building I had purchased for the training center down town. These two properties were in my name alone.

The elders made accusations against me that were founded on the jealousy of man and an inability to hear the direction of God. One man who had been given a voice convinced this group of leaders that I was a bad man. One man, whom we had trusted and made ourselves accountable to, instructed the leaders who served under me to write letters stating just what I had done to hurt them. Complaints ranged from an issue with a guitar to allegations that I didn't show enough appreciation. The man leading the rebellion filled over three pages with complaints about my lack of compassion and other charges. His list ended with placing a curse on my family and I stating that anything I touched would be eaten up with worms.

Then, everything became clear. I realized the plan of attack launched to destroy me, but it was too late. The man who had taken charge of the elders and deceived them into believing I was evil was the elder who had financial problems.

Again I turned to the man who watched for my soul. He was there to provide spiritual guidance and accountability. I felt that he would know what to do and instruct me accordingly. He directed me to write letters to these men repenting of my sin, whether it was real or not. This tore at my soul because I knew that all of this had come about because of my disobedience to God. I did not deal with the elder with the financial problem and his back-biting accusations because I did not want to be the bad guy. I wanted to please man, especially this man, but it was conflicting with the truth in my heart.

Ultimately, I chose to follow man without knowing the devastation that would follow my lack of faith and trust in God. The traitorous men took over the church under the same leadership I had looked to for guidance, and I become a coward in the sight of man. God had never released me from the work He had directed me to start.

SEALED FATE

With me out of the picture, the new leadership went right to work destroying any tie or connection to any part of the ministry I had touched. Although the church was free from debt, the men sold the land and the building and moved the church to another city. The rebuilding thrust the church into debt, and soon after, people began to leave. The money disappeared and monthly payments defaulted. In the end all the people scattered, the doors closed, and the work died.

I believe now that the last message I spoke concerning bitterness brought a level of accountability to the people and became the very thing that infected them. Bitterness in the leadership penetrated the people. People left hurt, unhappy, angry, and sad, but most of all they felt betrayed by me because I was the one who had stepped down. I did not want people to be angry with me, so I let other men take charge of what God had started—but He had never released me. Even today most of these people will have nothing to do with me even though changes have come to my life. This is the effect of bitterness and betrayal. Bitterness has a very strong and deep root. Be aware— it will destroy everything in your life.

MY SOLUTION

The resulting death of the church we had started was only one aspect of the situation. Alone, it was a devastating event, but along with it came personal affliction. The destruction to me and my family caused me to want to revert to my old nature and character. I had never been a coward in my life. Growing up, I was surrounded by liars and thieves. In my old lifestyle that type of person was a part of everyday living. Now, here in the church, I found myself surrounded by the same character of man—back-biters who would stab you in the back while smiling at your face. That aspect of religion had driven me away for years and now I was face to face with it again. I had never been a coward and would rather deal with men in the world where I could take care of business myself than fluff over them in church. Because of this betrayal, I was angry enough to walk away from God forever.

Every relationship I had built was affected by this betrayal. Other churches stopped associating with me. The ministry I had built fell apart because of my lack of faith and relationship with the Lord. Although the money was gone, the greater loss of wealth was the people we loved who did not love us anymore. I was no longer brother, friend, or pastor. I had now become "*Ron*," spoken with much disdain. My love, service, and sacrifice had been thrown back in my face like a dirty rag by close friends and even by people who had no direct interaction with me.

All this because I advised one man to walk what he talked and take care of his personal debts. Ironically, the true dialogue of his heart—betrayal, deception, and financial ruin—was the very path he chose to walk.

I internalized the pain of the betrayal. Day after day I went further inside the depths of hollow pain where I had been left to die. Then one day I knew what I had to do. I realized the action that would numb the ache and bring some sort of resolution—I would kill the elder who had destroyed everything I had built. They would put me in jail, but he had to pay for what he had done. As a young man, I had taken the lives of other men for committing far less personal pain. At the age of 20, I went to prison on three counts of murder, convicted to serve three consecutive terms of 25 to life. I was not afraid of the consequences. It simply was not in me to back down from a fight or to walk away from an attack. No, I had made up my mind that this man would pay for his actions.

Even though I had been pardoned by a ruling of self-defense and had walked upright with God and man for over 25 years, I had never been provoked to react with such an intense anger as I felt now. I felt that this was the only way to take care of the man who had betrayed me. He would pay for what he and the others had done to my family and the evil they had done to innocent people.

I was on my way to meet with the elder. The gun was loaded and my mind was set. The Father said, "Let it go." These words were not part of my vocabulary at that time so I traveled on, becoming angrier the farther I drove. My mind thundered with thoughts of revenge. He would pay with his life as I had paid; I would destroy him. Again, I heard the Father say, "Let it go. Ron, if you love me, let it go!" I stopped. The Father's love was stronger than my hatred for the man. I slowly turned the truck around and headed home.

This would make a nice "Hollywood" ending but the truth is that turning the truck around was just the first step down a long road back to hearing and knowing the heart of the Father. I went into a very deep depression. Because I was hated, I would be hateful. Believe me; I knew just how to hate. The only problem—my family received the hate and bitterness, not the men who had hurt me. At this point I was no good to anyone, not even to myself. I turned my face to the wall and left everything behind. Hours were spent sitting in my bedroom watching the news—not exactly a positive influence or spirit-lifting experience. I hurled my anger at the broadcasters in the box and dove deeper into the darkness.

Throughout this time, Minnie got a job while Ronda went to college and worked. I could not believe how they could go on with their lives while I was stuck in my self-pity. I was all alone and angrier than I had ever been in my life. I opened the door to satan and he walked in with all of his helpers. My hurt seemed to overrule anything my family was experiencing. Minnie would go on long walks and return with tears streaming down her cheeks. This would thrust the hurt deeper into my soul and I became even angrier with her. Soon Minnie and Ronda didn't have to do anything and I would be on them with a vengeance. All I could hear was my bitterness growing stronger and stronger, drowning out the Voice that was saying, "Ron, I love you."

My Choice

Then, a new voice began to rise up in my spirit. Questions rolled over in my mind relentlessly. How could this have happened to me? Where was God now in my time of need? I began to believe that I was no good and would be better off dead than in this place of torment. So, I decided to fill my hand with something all too familiar—cold, hard steel. Only this time, I had become the enemy of destruction and betrayal. I took the gun and headed to the place where I had prayed throughout my ministry. I believed that I was no good and no longer had any value. My heart was full of bitterness. This was a worse hell than I had ever experienced, but I knew how to make it stop.

As I sat alone in the truck, I put the loaded gun in my mouth and pulled the trigger. The empty click echoed loudly in the stillness. In frustration, I pointed the gun out the window and pulled the trigger, shooting off five rounds. I threw the gun to the truck floor while crying out to God, "I can't even kill myself! Why?" The small voice I had skillfully learned to silence in the darkness now whispered, "Ron, I love you." Time stood still in the truck on that hilltop overlooking the city. I knew I could not walk away from God's love any longer but I still had no direction to help me out of where I had placed myself.

I went back to my family and began seeking God. I did not know where to go but I knew I had already stayed in the lap of betrayal and bitterness far too long. I moved my family out of our huge home into a small garage with the dream of building a home. The house was not built so we lived in the garage for several years.

I started buying and selling cars, and we opened a detail shop where I could use my prison training. We worked all day and into the night. It was a good business that kept us busy. Even though it was not exactly what I had promised Minnie when we were married, at least we were far removed from those so-called "good" people.

GOD'S PLAN

Through time, God brought men into my life who began to pull on the treasures He had placed in my heart. I decided to go to a place called the Slab to minister to the homeless, the drunks, the street people—those who had been left to die, just like me. We were all pretty much in the same boat. None of us had much hope or dreams for the future. For a year, I spoke to these people, and they helped me more than I helped them.

My heart began to soften to the Voice that I had heard for so many years, but I still would not let go of the hurt. During that time seven individuals prophesied that God would do greater things in my life, but the words seemed empty to me. All the hurt and bitterness stored inside me had festered like a cancer. I wanted nothing to do with Christianity because men in my past had done evil to me—they were no more like Christ than I was.

Still, one statement from one of the prophecies broke through the tears of my heart and I can still hear it today: "Satan has placed you in a coffin. He is nailing the lid closed and is ready to bury you but God says, 'It shall not be so.' He has removed the nails and lifted the lid. He placed His hands under your arms and raised you up and shook the death clothes from you. He says, 'I will place your feet on good soil and you shall plow in My field and you shall never plow alone.' Put the wall down and I will place you on your destiny."

I heard those words like a charge of electricity over a newly-live wire. When I truly realized that He was not finished with me, His loved flowed over me like rushing floodwaters. I was changed instantly, in a moment. In one breath I knew He was still there and purpose surged through my spirit.

A year or so passed and I found myself looking for more. I had a promise and I wanted to get started as soon as possible. Today, I am actively doing what God has called me to do. I have learned a lot about betrayal from the personal pain of experience. The hardest part of moving forward is the most necessary ingredient—vulnerability. I had to tear down the wall of protection and become open to the possibility of hurt. That is not always easy. When it gets tough, I remember back to that small Voice that says, "Ron, I love you." Then, I pull up on my bootstraps and away we go!

I have learned that I am not a *victim* of betrayal. Betrayal is what I did to God in Heaven. It is what brother does to brother. Betrayal can cause mental, spiritual, and emotional death, but when you begin to see betrayal as a teacher, rather than a death sentence, you will emerge victorious.

As you read through this book, my prayer is that if you have been betrayed you will find answers to overcome. If you have been a betrayer, I pray for a change of heart. The end result of betrayal in your life is your choice—whether life-changing or life-ending. Choose life. Actually, choose abundant life. There are many situations of betrayal that we all go through that are too painful to even think about. But please realize that betrayal is like a stone in a riverbed that can be smoothed and soothed by the rushing water of God's love.

Chapter 2

PROCESS OF BETRAYAL

Betrayal is the manifestation of something much greater—an internal hurt that lies invisible on the surface but digs deeply into the core of a person. When you look at a tree, the trunk, limbs, and leaves are easily visible but the taproot is deep underground, hidden from the naked eye. The root of betrayal is often buried deep as well, covered with mounds of emotions or self-imposed manipulations to keep it hidden. Because of this, betrayal can be dangerously fatal to your emotional, spiritual, and psychological being. While the tree's taproot provides nourishment for life, the root of betrayal releases poison and bitterness for death.

If we learn to see betrayal for what it is, we will walk as overcomers. Our enemy, satan, uses a process of betrayal as a tactic of destruction. This single act can consume us to the point where everything we view, everything we say, and all of our actions derive from the point of betrayal. Through the established character of Christ in our lives we can stop this process and kill the root so that betrayal never infiltrates our heart or latches onto our lives.

What does it mean to betray? We have all experienced the feeling of being betrayed to some degree. It can be as simple as a salesperson choosing someone else in line to move in front of us or as complicated as the severing of a marriage. To *betray* is to "give over," either in the sense of delivering a person or thing to be kept by another or to deliver to prison or judgment. Betrayal gleans its power from the destruction of trust, the quest for self-will, and a web of deception. It is generally looked at as a treacherous act done by a betrayer, a traitor. We see this title given to Judas in Luke 6:16, but Judas was not the first to betray.

Betrayal started in the very beginning, in the heavens, and we are still experiencing the residual effect of that act today. The very first betrayal happened between satan and the Father. Satan decided that he would rule over God and convinced a third of the angels that he was capable of successfully achieving his goal. His deception was so powerful that none of the angels who chose to go with him turned away, even after the Father confronted satan and threw him out of Heaven. Satan said in his heart:

> ...*I will ascend to heaven; I will raise my throne above the stars of God, And I will sit on the mount of assembly in the recesses of the north. I will ascend above the heights of the clouds; I will make myself like the Most High* (Isaiah 14:13-14).

Satan's scheme employed lying, deceiving, and making accusations in an effort to manipulate his position. Today he uses the same process of betrayal to build walls between family members, rip apart congregations, and destroy covenant relationships. If we are going to overcome any past or future betrayals in our life, we must understand the nature of the one who originated the act of betrayal.

SATAN'S CHARACTER—HE IS A LIAR

The nature of God is as far removed from the nature of satan as light is from darkness. God is truth and there is no deceit in Him. This is a vital concept to grasp because we must understand there is no way that God could ever be the source of any betrayal. Satan is a liar and the truth cannot be found anywhere in his nature. It is clear in the following Scripture what we are dealing with when we choose to walk in lies.

> *You are of your father the devil, and you want to do the desires of your father. He was a murderer from the beginning, and does not stand in the truth, because there is no truth in him. Whenever he speaks a lie, he speaks from his own nature; for he is a liar, and the father of lies* (John 8:44).

Lying is as much a part of satan's make-up as blood is to the human body. It flows throughout him; it fuels him to function. Matthew 16:13 is a perfect example of how quickly satan can illusively slip into a situation by presenting a lie, which we in turn can use to position ourselves or our own will. In this passage of Scripture, Jesus has asked His disciples who the people say he is. They tell Him that the people have responded by naming several different individuals. Then He asks the disciples, *"Who do you say that I am?"*

> *Simon Peter answered: "You are the Christ, the Son of the living God." And Jesus said to him, "Blessed are you, Simon Barjona, because flesh and blood did not reveal this to you, but my Father who is in heaven"* (Matthew 16:16-17).

Jesus praised Simon Peter because he had correctly discerned the truth by the Spirit of God. Peter had received a visitation of the Father and identity had come into his life. Christ gave him the keys to the Kingdom because of his divine revelation. Those keys would unlock the destiny and purpose in Peter's life (see Matthew 16:19). This was the perfect time to plant a lie that would turn the sincere approval of God into a point of pride. How easy it is to become puffed up when we feel validated by God or even through the accolades of man. Satan did not look at Peter's commendation and back away thinking he was too close to the Son of God—he came in for the kill, planting the presumption of Peter's agenda above Jesus' purpose. As they walk along, Jesus foretells His own death. This same disciple that was to be given the keys of the Kingdom now turns around, takes Jesus to the side, and begins to rebuke Him. In verse 23 of the same chapter in Matthew Jesus responds:

> *"Get behind Me, Satan! You are a stumbling block to Me; for you are not setting your mind on God's interests, but man's"* (Matthew 16:23).

In this example Peter is betraying Christ because he does not see the value of Jesus' death. Jesus tells Peter that what he has done has become a stumbling block. Satan had deceived Peter into thinking that he had the right answer and that Christ was in error. Peter had set his agenda above God's and made it his responsibility to set the matter straight. Do you see the betrayal? It is amazing that when betrayal comes into our life we want to take control and change circumstances to fit the way we believe they should be, or we try to correct people and change their identity to what we feel is right for them. Most of the time it is because we want to establish our own will. This is the birthplace of betrayal.

Recently, a woman asked me if I thought that a person who betrays someone is acting intentionally. My answer: most of the time I do not believe they are acting intentionally. In my experience, many people are genuinely trying to help. Sometimes in betrayal the person does not know exactly what your heart is in a situation or what you are trying to accomplish. From their perspective they think they have the right answer. Without trying to understand the strategies of your heart, they try to change the way you are working it out to their way. This begins a series of actions or changes that are in opposition to yours. Lies of the deceiver have led them down the path to becoming a betrayer.

Our human nature, or "gut feeling," generally kicks in when we face a situation that doesn't seem quite right. We try to correct, adjust, or rebuke the person we see to be in error according to our viewpoint. Christ recognized that this response from Peter came from his human or fallen nature; that is why He spoke directly to satan. When I was asked to step down from the church and the network of churches I had built, I believed that I was doing the right thing. In reality, my action was a stumbling block because it did not carry out the mandate of the Father's will for my life.

Betrayal is not isolated to a people group, religion, or culture; there are many examples even in the business world. Many of you may be able to relate to being offered a management position on the condition that you first work your way up through the ranks, starting out as a salesperson. With the promise of advancement, you accept the sales job knowing that it is only for a short time. After three months on the floor, instead of being promoted to management someone from outside of the company accepts the job that should have been given to you. To drive the knife in deeper, your manager asks you to stay on as a salesperson because you do such a great job—with no increase in pay and no promise of advancement. What you *do* gain is a feeling of betrayal: you have been lied to, deceived, and cheated. As the employer removes his hand from the knife, you take hold of it, thrusting it deeper while you say, "What did I do? What is wrong with me?"

Whether it is in corporate America or at the local market, employers everywhere present a truth to attract candidates and then retract the truth as if there is no consequence. During the process the employer may have hired someone who was more qualified, the financial situation may have changed, or they were being intentionally deceptive from the start. Either way, the end result is the same: you feel betrayed and a deep seed of bitterness has been thrown on the soil of your heart. To some in the business world this type of behavior is considered good business. In His Kingdom, it is wrong. And to the individual, it can be extremely damaging.

Satan uses lies to establish self-will that causes us to correct what we view to be in error, and to accept lies that are actually empty promises. Every pendulum swings toward two extremes. In my own life, lies were used in an effort to compromise truth. In situations where true error was addressed by the moving of the Holy Spirit, truth was challenged. As a young minister I was told that I was too tough, too straightforward. "You need to be more gentle," became an all too familiar comment. Then people would try to "help" me by referring me to Scriptures like: *"Rejoice in the Lord always; again I will say rejoice! Let your gentle spirit be known to all men. The Lord is near"* (Phil. 4:4-5).

I felt that men who did not know, or even care to know, the cry of my heart were telling me to compromise the truth as I knew it so that I would be more approachable, more likeable. They used this Scripture, emphasizing the word "gentle," so that I would compromise and stop addressing difficult issues. This was the first step on a path that would lead to my betrayal. However, if I had gone along with the crowd, I would have been the betrayer of God's purposes for the believers He had entrusted me with.

Over the years and through many painful experiences, I have come to realize that a gentle or forbearing spirit does not mean that you do not deal with truth in a problem or situation. It only means that you are able to be understanding and sympathetic while dealing with the tough issues so that change can come. Whether we read about Jesus, Peter, Paul, or other apostles, all of them used a forbearing spirit to deal with the sin nature of people. Then, they were willing to wait and allow the work of the Spirit to be accomplished. If we do not compromise the truth when attempting to sincerely help change someone's character for the better, God's refining fire is released to work and fulfill His destiny in that person's life.

In First Corinthians 5:1-5, Paul is writing to church leadership who have compromised truth and refused to deal with a situation of immorality. He tells them that their actions have caused them to become arrogant. Paul is more concerned about the soul of the man being saved than the flesh of the man being hurt.

It is reported commonly that there is fornication among you, and such fornication as is not so much as named among the Gentiles, that one should have his father's wife. And ye are puffed up, and have not rather mourned, that he that hath done this deed might be taken away from among you. For I verily, as absent in body, but present in spirit, have judged already, as though I were present, concerning him that hath so done this deed, in the name of our Lord Jesus Christ, when ye are gathered together, and my spirit, with the power of our Lord Jesus Christ, to deliver such an one unto Satan for the destruction of the flesh, that the spirit may be saved in the day of the Lord Jesus (1 Corinthians 5:1-5).

Today, like the leaders of old, we continue to look the other way and choose to just accept people the way they are because we do not want to hurt their feelings. The lie that people will be better off if we say nothing is a primary tool of the enemy. Compromise never helps truth and never brings healing.

No matter how good it may sound at the moment, a lie is never your friend. It will only ultimately bring division in any relationship you have. Relationship is based on what you are—what you say—what you do. It is either a reflection of God's nature being revealed or satan's nature of fallen man. When relationships are filled with any degree of lying, satan's nature is coming to bear in that relationship. The root of betrayal has been planted.

SATAN'S CHARACTER—HE IS A DECEIVER

In every situation, we are led either by the Spirit or the flesh. With a world of information streaming through radio, television, and Internet, rightly discerning the Word of Truth can be challenging. In so many areas of life, the enemy has used deception in an effort to lead us into a false paradigm so the line between reality and perception becomes faded. A controversial example is the removal of Christ from Christmas. Christmas has become a holiday celebration filled with guidelines about what decorations or greetings are acceptable and will not offend. The reality of Christ's birth and resurrection has been washed over with themes of diversity and equality resulting in a lie wrapped in nice packaging so that everyone (except Christians) will be more comfortable.

Deceiving someone is different than lying to them. Although many deceptions start with a lie, deception is much more elaborate. It involves skillful misleading—the right mixture of truth, lies, and omission of truth. These elements are crafted together to paint a picture of perception that will affect the way we respond.

In Matthew 4:3-10, satan twists Scripture in an attempt to manipulate Jesus' responses. The Spirit of God led Jesus into the wilderness. This passage is famous for teaching believers down through the centuries to overcome temptation, but it is so much richer than that one aspect. Jesus was sure of His identity, He knew His purpose, and He walked having the mindset of God. The wilderness was a battlefield of the mind of God versus the deceptive mind of fallen man. In a place of physical weakness, satan tried to manipulate Jesus through deception in order to make Him do something contrary to the heart of God. In a time of vulnerability, the enemy tried to lure Jesus with fraudulent promises of sustenance, identity, and power.

Deception is a useful tool for attacking one's identity. Here in the wilderness, satan uses portions of Scripture to challenge the identity of Christ—he uses this same tactic against us today. Twice he says to Jesus, *"If you are the Son of God..."* [make the stones bread, throw yourself down]." Jesus responds with the full truth of Scripture, dispelling the "reality" the enemy was trying to create (see Matthew 4:3-10). Jesus was a mature man, carrying destiny and purpose within Him. When satan said, *"If you are the Son of God,"* he was trying to make Jesus doubt the words of the Father. He attacked the reasoning of Christ just as he had attacked Adam's reasoning in the Garden with the words, "surely God did not mean..." (see Genesis 3:1-8).

If Jesus had submitted to the attack of the enemy, satan would have taken over His identity and immediately gone to accuse Him before the Father. Here in the wilderness, Jesus overcame satan by trusting in the infallible Word of God and staying secure in who He is. Through the confrontation, the Father's mindset was solidified in the Son.

Every one of us can relate to a wilderness experience we have had at some point in our lives. In the lonely place of betrayal, the enemy uses the emotional distress in an effort to upset the mind of God in us. When we are betrayed, our identity becomes blurred and hazy. We begin to doubt who we are and will cling to whatever truth we trust. All it takes is surrendering to one lie and a cloud of deception begins to form around us. From that tiny lie, our path to destiny is altered. We begin to walk out into areas where God never intended us to go.

In a place of vulnerability, our humanity begins to scream, "There's no hope, there is no way out." From this faulty altered status, we begin to notice the cracks and start to break down. We question what we have done wrong or how we could have failed so miserably. It is here where deception begins to fully manifest itself. Satan's entire process of betrayal is based on your deception. The tempter will take twisted and manipulated truth and begin to form accusations against you.

Many times, the enemy's weapons of warfare are disguised as the ones you trust and love the most. We have all heard, "Keep your loved ones close and your enemies closer." The truth is that an enemy will rarely betray you in a manner that impacts your life or causes you to veer off course. Only those you are vulnerable with, those you trust, have the full power to come in close enough to cut through your defenses. Whether they come from others or you begin to charge yourself with accusations, the devastation is the same. Betrayal will build up the betrayer and diminish the one being betrayed.

Sometimes we become vulnerable with people not because they have been grafted into our hearts but because of their position in our lives. There is a natural feeling of security that comes when you submit to an authority figure. In various degrees we accept counsel, correction, or advice from these figures, and if we become hurt in the process a sense of betrayal surrounds the distress. Our trust becomes shaken. In truth, the situation is exposing the fact that our trust has been leveraged on a weak foundation—man.

In Genesis, Adam chose to place his trust in humanity when he chose the creation over the Creator and betrayed God in the Garden. He was driven to preserve his human destiny more than his spiritual destiny. Satan utilized every tool of craftiness to mislead Adam and Eve and he still uses them against us today. The enemy will come after what God has created in you and for you, trying to deceive you into believing that his plan is better than God's original design.

> *But I am afraid that, as the serpent deceived Eve by his craftiness, your minds will be led astray from the simplicity and purity of devotion to Christ* (2 Corinthians 11:3).

The deceiver attacks your thought process by cloaking betrayal in truth. This intrusion leads you away from uncomplicated, undefiled intimacy with Christ through a false promise of self-preservation. When you find yourself wrought with the excruciating pain of betrayal, your natural human instinct is to run away, shut down, or wrap yourself behind walls of seclusion. The deception is that isolation will be comforting. In the safety of being alone, you will be able to stop the voices, the torment, the pain. It is in wrapping yourself with these very lies that you separate yourself from the healing simplicity of Christ and life becomes more complicated. You are pushed into the wilderness, removed from God, and the accusations begin to churn around you.

SATAN'S CHARACTER—HE IS THE ACCUSER

Accusation is a statement against character. Whether it is true or untrue, a statement of accusation has the power to make you classify yourself as a failure. In moments of feeling like you have failed, condemnation grabs hold of your heart and your confidence is shaken. You begin to look at every situation and relationship in a different light. Once you realize you have been betrayed, you feel like you must have failed everyone in every way because you have fallen suspect to betrayal.

We are in an all-out war and it surrounds our daily life. We fight one another thinking they are the enemy. We put up walls of survival to try and ward off any future betrayals. Inside the walls, accusation continues day and night. This is because there is a real enemy making accusation against you continually and it beats against your life in the spirit realm and the natural.

> ...For the accuser of our brethren has been thrown down, he who accuses them before our God day and night (Revelation 12:10).

Satan is looking for a way to ensnare you. He tries to tell God that man does not trust Him. Then he turns around and tells man that he cannot trust God. All he needs is one party to take hold of the accusation and a crack of division will form. A powerful Scripture example of this satan-induced circumstance is found in the Book of Job. God declares Job to be a blameless man. Satan brings an accusation that Job trusted God only because he had been blessed with great wealth and possessions. At that point, God gave satan permission to bring trials to Job's life, with the only condition being to spare his life (see Job 1-42).

The trying of Job began. We know from Scripture that he was a very wealthy man with a large family. Over time, everything was taken from Job—family, health, lands, and material possessions. Friends began to draw back and fall away. He was criticized and beaten down. Assassination attempts were hurled at his character and he found himself all alone.

Still, Job was not isolated because he never turned his back on God. He cried out to God and he questioned the events but in the end his trust was so firmly seared in God that he would not bow to the accusations of the enemy coming through those around him. Even when his own wife told him to curse God and die, Job refused to let what looked like the betrayal of God overturn the reality of his trust in God.

If we do not understand the process of betrayal we will continue to repeat the cycle. You cannot travel in the same direction and expect to arrive at a totally different destination. When you continually follow the same process or same path, you end up with the same betrayal.

Betrayal manifests through many different means—rumors, jealousy, greed, and others. Regardless of how it begins, it hurts. A dividing line separates those who believe the accusation and those who do not. Invisible lines are formed causing segregation that reaches far beyond the two individuals involved.

Have you ever stayed at home instead of going to church or a meeting simply because of others who might have been there? After the sting of betrayal, the person who betrayed you can easily be magnified into a people group or idea. You stay home and reject having any part of Christianity because someone from a church hurt you. You feel betrayed by a co-worker and the job becomes a place where you mentally separate those who are on "your side" from those on your accuser's side.

Accusations can quickly result in condemnation. When we realize the extent to which betrayal destroys others and us, we begin to notice when condemnation enters in and quickly check to make sure any access point for betrayal or accusations is sealed off. Condemnation is also a checkpoint for us to notice when we are walking outside of faith in our relationship to God.

> *Therefore there is now no condemnation for those who are in Christ Jesus. For the law of the Spirit of life in Christ Jesus has set you free from the law of sin and of death* (Romans 8:1-2).

Christ overcame betrayal and reestablished freedom from sin and death. What was taken away in the Garden was given back through the blood of Jesus Christ. Jesus recognized the lies and the deceit of the enemy. He overcame the accuser. We have been set free completely from the stronghold of condemnation. Because Christ overcame, we as children of God have been given the power to overcome. We have been set free from the law of sin and death, including the death attempts of betrayal. The Spirit of God can set you free from the condemnation of humanity.

> *We shall know by this that we are of the truth, and will assure our heart before Him, in whatever our heart condemns us; for God is greater than our heart, and knows all things* (1 John 3:19-20).

The nature of satan—to lie, deceive, and accuse—can be fully manifested through the process of betrayal. Once you are betrayed, you will betray others. The cycle repeats without end unless you allow God to rid you of the pain of betrayal. Only the restoration of God's nature—the nature of love—can completely defeat betrayal.

You do not have to fall victim to the workings of satan's nature. With his nature exposed, you can begin to safeguard against the enemy's schemes. The consuming jealousy that drives him to torment man, God's beloved creation, with the very act that he himself once used to try to position himself over the Father fuels the deeds he practices against man. The outworking of those deeds is always to steal, kill, and destroy.

Satan's Acts: To Steal, Kill, and Destroy

We know that Christ has overcome the evil one and given us the authority over satan. We are able to walk in this power through relationship. It is also relationship that shields us against satan's lies, deceptive ploys, and accusations.

> *So Jesus said to them again, "Truly, truly, I say to you, I am the door of the sheep. All who came before Me are thieves and robbers, but the sheep did not hear them"* (John 10:7-8).

If we maintain close relationship with Jesus, satan can come after us but he has no authority over us. As His sheep, we do not have to accept the lies of the enemy. Our personal relationship with Jesus dispels the fraudulent claims of the enemy because the Truth resides within us. Our disposition becomes the same one that Job portrayed: they may slay me but I will still praise Him. Job knew his source was the Father in Heaven not himself or others.

Relationship goes far beyond salvation. We enter in through the Door, Jesus Christ, but that is just the beginning of a walk full of winding paths, unpredictable terrain, and fluctuating atmospheres. In the midst of this wild and wonderful journey, a very real adversary is seeking our destruction.

> *I am the door; If anyone enters through Me, he will be saved, and shall go in and out, and find pasture. The thief comes only to steal and kill, and destroy...* (John 10:9-10).

From the moment you accept Jesus as Lord of your life, you are impregnated with the righteousness, peace, and joy of Father God. His Kingdom is implanted in you to strengthen you to the point where it becomes manifested in your life. Then it can begin to be released into everyone around you so that the love of God reaches the ends of the earth.

Satan is out to steal, kill, and destroy any expression of the character of God in your life. Through trickery, accusations, and betrayal, he relentlessly searches for those he determines to be easy prey. What you must understand is that as a child of God, you are surrounded by the presence of God. No matter where we are, He is with us whether it is in a barren, isolated valley or on a magnificent mountain top.

Why then do we feel so alone at times, especially in the midst of a struggle? According to First Corinthians 1:18, we are *"being saved."* It is a process, not a one-time episode of emotional outpouring. We need to work out our salvation as it says in Philippians 2:12 and pursue the answer for our struggles. All of the answers are in the Word of God and in us changing every day through the power of that Word. When your mind is transformed by the Word, the knowledge of Christ enables you to recognize and disclose the wayward attempts of satan.

Satan seeks to destroy something very specific in your life— your provision. Automatically, many people relate this to monetary currency but the provision Christ secured for us is much more valuable than paper money and precious metals.

> *I am the good shepherd; the good Shepherd lays down His life for the sheep* (John 10:11).

In laying down His life, Jesus is our example for walking through betrayal. Satan has come to take away that provision made through Christ in an effort to stop our relationship with

God the Father. The Kingdom of God is at hand and satan does not want you to see the truth of the life that was laid down for you. The power of the sacrifice enables you to lay down whatever has come against you and allows the love of Christ to be made manifest in you. This alone stops the cycle of betrayal.

> *Therefore let us not judge one another anymore, but rather determine this—not to put an obstacle or a stumbling block in a brother's way* (Romans 14:13).

SATAN'S PURSUIT—YOUR RIGHTEOUSNESS, PEACE, AND JOY

The thief comes to steal, kill and destroy our righteousness, peace and joy, the very essence of the relationship between God and man.

> *For the kingdom of God is not eating or drinking, but righteousness, and peace and joy in the Holy Spirit* (Romans 14:17).

Righteousness, peace, and joy—these are three principles of the Kingdom of God. When you find that doing things as Christ would is no longer part of your life, this is an indication that you have been listening to the lies of satan. When peace cannot be found, satan has deceived you into frustration. The final blow is the elimination of joy. You find that you are unhappy with everyone and everything. Your life is totally upside down. You don't know whether you are coming or going, or even if you have left yet. I have found myself in that state many times and it is not enjoyable.

A few years ago, our son-in-law and daughter welcomed their second child into the world. Every time I spoke with my daughter on the phone, she would say, "I just can't get anything done; if it's not Abby, it's John Luke. They are taking up all my time. I clean up mess after mess. Abby won't sleep through the night. I am tired all the time." She was trapped in an atmosphere of frustration and stress.

Our accomplished, talented daughter had begun to take in the lies of the enemy and believe that she was unproductive and ineffective. The accusations of the enemy against her, through her own mind, were causing her to try and convince others of her ineffectual state. Her husband would come home from work and try to help, but they were both being dragged down the path of lies together.

Soon, the lies of the enemy began to manifest as a bad attitude toward the children because nothing was getting done. The tired and busy mom had entered into a full state of deception. The final mark of the enemy's plan was the removal of joy from the home. John Luke was always on her nerves. All Abigail could do was cry and they both wanted more attention then she could give. Now all three of them were crying. Where was the laughter? What had happened to this loving, giving, joyous family that I had seen just a few months earlier?

Realize that this is how subtle the works of the enemy are in our lives. Because the thief had a place to accuse her, her perception was that she was incapable of getting anything done. Joy had totally left their lives. Condemnation was having its full effect. The struggle going on inside of my daughter spilled over onto everyone in the household.

While we were talking, I began to share all that she had accomplished in that day alone. She could not believe that she had done so much. Her eyes and heart began to open and the thief lost his stronghold. Righteousness, peace, and joy filled her heart and surged cheerfully through her home once again.

Our enemy is real and we must recognize that he is coming after us with a vengeance. It's not the trials that control us, it's how we react when we face the trials. Joy is our strength to overcome through the Holy Spirit.

It is not the trials that control us, it is how we react when we face the trials.

SATAN EXPOSED

From the moment satan decided that he could rule Heaven and the ploy of betrayal entered his heart to deceive man and turn Jesus against the Father, satan's nature has always been destructive. When you understand his nature, the acts he employs to carry out his nature, and the purpose of his pursuit, you will be better equipped to stand against this enemy. The following diagram helps identify the workings of the evil one against God's children.

Nature:	Liar	Deceiver	Accuser
Acts:	Steals	Kills	Destroys
Pursuit:	Righteousness	Peace	Joy

A lie steals your righteousness, when you are deceived it kills your peace, and when you are accused your joy is destroyed. You are no longer able to stand erect as a man or woman of God. Yielding to these weapons enables the enemy to wipe away any integrity that you have in Christ.

Satan has had countless centuries to perfect his tactics. Our only course of study for understanding the results of betrayal comes from the examples we see in others and the example Christ gave us. It is up to you to decide which example you will follow. What will your example be to your children? Will satan rule your house as a result of the betrayal you have experienced or even caused? May it never be so! If you will allow your intimacy with Christ to become strong, then the love of God for everyone will be evidenced in overcoming your trials and tribulations.

Chapter 3

SLIPPERY IDENTITY

Who am I? What am I supposed to do? Where am I going? Why was I even born? These are the questions I asked myself as I sat in that truck on the dusty road, holding the gun in my hand. When we find ourselves caught up in conflict, our perception of the value of what we are becomes greatly diminished. We do not see anything as it truly is because our focus is centered on the fact that our life is in turmoil.

As a general rule, people do not like being unhappy. When problems seem to overtake us, our first reaction is usually not one of embracing the crisis as a training tool or seeing it as an opportunity for growth. We fail to remember that challenges and difficulties teach us the right and wrong way of accomplishing given tasks. Very quickly our identity becomes wrapped up in a negative cycle of reacting to the stress that surrounds us.

A Life Based on Works

Minnie and I travel a great deal while ministering across the United States. Do you remember being on a road trip when things did not go quite as you expected? Well, magnify that memory about 100 times because of the size and mechanical complexities of a motorcoach, and that's what we face. Driving across America in a coach exposes you to all kinds of traffic, inattentive drivers, unexpected delays, miles of roadwork, and mechanical malfunctions.

There have been times when it would have been easy for my identity to become caught up in keeping the coach going or staying on schedule but I would have missed the very purpose for which God told me to travel in the first place—ministering to church leaders. My identity has to be centered on sharing the Father's heart, not on what it takes for me to physically arrive at a location.

For too long, the believer's walk with Christ has been based on works. Success for leaders in ministry arrives when a large empire is built around their own particular charismatic personality, and numbers and resources drive public opinion about the effectiveness of a church or pastor. On the lay level, many church members aspire to be like the people who sing in the choir, teach Sunday School, or are asked to sit on a committee.

God's cry has never been for churches to add a "contemporary" service to their schedule or for a believer to spend every Saturday night vacuuming the sanctuary. Hear me—having a heart to serve is important and your acts of service to God are never in vain when they are birthed in a desire to please Him, driven by obedience and passion for a Savior who paid your debt and lives now to intercede for you. Sacrifice or service without passion or obedience is just dead works. It is unacceptable to a holy God because it is driven out of lack of identity.

Scripture shows us a man whose identity was caught up in the works behind a sacrifice rather than the obedience of the offering. In Genesis chapter 4, we see where God regarded the offering that Able presented but rejected Cain's offering. In verse 6, the Lord spoke to Cain about the nature of his sacrifice, which resulted in his fallen countenance.

> *Then the Lord said to Cain, "Why are you angry? And why has your countenance fallen? If you do well will not your countenance be lifted up? And if you do not do well, sin is crouching at the door; and its desire is for you, but you must master it"* (Genesis 4:6-7).

God was telling Cain that there was a need for intimacy between them. Cain had the same opportunity as Abel but his sacrifice was made out of obligation and works rather than identity and intimacy. The far-reaching love of God instructed Cain how to make the sacrifice acceptable, but Cain's jealousy of Abel drove him to reject God's instruction and his identity slipped away. Cain's disobedience culminated in an act of betrayal against Abel and ultimately led to his own destruction.

When you have an intimate relationship with Christ, problems and situations can be viewed from the proper perspective. Intimacy with the Father gives you identity in eternity so that you can view situations in your life through a larger, clearer lens. Issues that seem too large to handle are cut down to size when you understand that there is nothing so grave that the blood of Jesus cannot overcome it. When the problems of life grip you, joy and peace easily slip away like water through your fingers. Your countenance, or physical expression, drops and you find that sin is crouching at the door waiting to overtake you.

A clear and powerful example of this in our everyday lives is when you tell a child, "No." Almost immediately, his expression or attitude changes because he did not get his way. As adults, we are not so different. Many times, when events appear contrary to our expectations, we react the same way. We have been given ability to overcome, but overcoming is a choice. Only intimacy with Jesus can drive us to the right choice; identity must be found in Him.

> *I have been crucified with Christ; and it is no longer I who live, but Christ lives in me; and the life which I now live in the flesh I live by faith in the Son of God, who loved me, and delivered Himself up for me* (Galatians 2:20).

The simplicity of this verse can become clouded as it is taken from the written text and put into application because it is not just you and Christ alone in the world. Life is full of other people and you have to deal with their attitudes and character every day. Sometimes people or things begin to define our character, watering down the pure power of Christ's life within us.

I am sure that each of us could quickly come up with a short list of people or outside influences making an impact on our lives. Whether we truly realize it or not, television, magazines, and media of all sorts tell us what we should be like and how we are to act. Other people willingly offer their opinion or advice about how you should act and think, and even process information. Society says that in order to be successful, you must graduate from college and land a great job. Some define success as starting your own business. Whatever the given criteria, it seems that Christ never even enters the picture because being "God-centered" is not a popular requirement for today's lifestyle.

Before I became God-centered, the right way to do something was *my* way. I did not care if people knew who they were, as long as they knew for certain that I was someone to be feared. My experience from walking through so much of the world's ways has taught me that people do not always have the right answers. People will make you into the image they have for you, but Christ has already called you for a specific purpose. Every person on earth has been placed here to accomplish the fullness of life in Christ. God wants you to touch this earth with His presence.

> *I will put My law within them and on their heart I will write it; and I will be their God, and they shall be My people* (Jeremiah 31:33).

If you look back over your life, you can probably remember a time when if felt as if you had a hole in your heart—an emptiness that could not be filled with a better job, a greater social standing, or anything else. There was an ache, like some part of you was missing. Maybe you are experiencing that ache even now. Keep reading, realizing your identity is a crucial step in enjoying a fulfilled, abundant life.

At one time, I had a hole in my heart. It almost seems more appropriate to say that I had a heart within a massive hole in my life. When I accepted Christ, the hole was filled. Countless others have spoken of the same emptiness in themselves and the treasure of having Christ fill that void. Because of the fallen nature of man, we are born into humanity without the Spirit of Christ. The Spirit of God is the only One who can fill that empty place in man where there is no direction, no destiny, and no purpose.

I was 26 years old when Christ came into my life. For the first time I began to realize that there was a reason for me to be here. I did have a purpose and destiny beyond anything my lifestyle dictated for me. Even though there were things in my life that I should not have done, my purpose and calling were steadfast in

Christ. I began to seek the Father's heart in order to find the exact direction He had for me.

Apostle Paul talks about not doing the things we should do and doing those things that we should not do (see Romans 7:15-20). It is the classic struggle of man as he balances between the spirit and the flesh. We have all experienced this struggle because no one is exempt from the snare of the enemy. The fall of mankind in the Garden sealed the fate that we are all born into sin, searching for God. Realizing the nature of our true identity in Christ can be difficult. As we walk through the process of our actions and choices, the Spirit of God can teach us who we are on a consistent, everyday basis.

When I first became saved, I knew that I could change the world because of what Jesus had done. I set out with a fiery passion to blaze a trail of glory. As I began to learn the intricacies of how this walk worked, I began to understand that it is not as easy as I had thought. There were deeds written in the Word of God that I could not do because of my own character flaws. I did not have the ability to see past my faults, let alone the faults of others who called themselves Christians.

Through time and the structuring of God, I have realized that any good in me is not really me, it is Christ. I am learning to have patience with others, allowing them to change even as I have been allowed to grow and change by those who labored in love with me. If we can come together in that unity of the faith, Christ will work in us to touch the world. People will truly know us by our love one for another.

When we labor in our own strength, apart from one another, to build our personal houses, many times they are built on jealousy, anger, and bitterness. At the very best, building in our own strength produces weak structures comprised of past experiences.

We must stop relying on our own frail ability—allowing our identity in Him to slip away. For years, we have done things wrong, yet we continue to work the same process hoping for a different outcome. This is insanity that leads to naught.

The process of building Christ's character in our lives is to submit to God, resist our flesh, and walk in love. Every Christian knows that unless we allow the Lord to build His character in us, our own fleshly labor is in vain. Each of us is a house that Jesus is building—His worth is showcased to the world through our lives. This is why a fundamental building block to finding your identity is focusing on Christ. If we fix our eyes on Him, He will build the house.

SEARCHING FOR COMPLETENESS

When we honestly look at where we are today, it is clear that we are far from God's complete plan for us. The sinful nature of fallen man has corrupted a world created for His glory. Our future is very grim through the eyes of mankind. Although we all know that the end is coming, we don't know how soon. So to have any hope of providing an answer for tomorrow, we need a solution to the struggles of today.

> *But realize this, that in the last days difficult times will come. For men will be lovers of self, lovers of money, boastful, arrogant, revilers, disobedient to parents, ungrateful, unholy, unloving, irreconcilable, malicious gossips, without self-control, brutal, haters of good, treacherous, reckless, conceited, lovers of pleasure rather than lovers of God; holding to a form of godliness, although they have denied its power; and avoid such men as these* (2 Timothy 3:1-5).

This passage of Scripture is a realistically gripping excerpt that could easily headline a nightly news program. It is one of those Scriptures that we read over very quickly, hoping that everything will work out just fine in the end. We want the world to change without making the sacrifice that change will require.

In the solitude of reflection, each of us can identify with the character traits listed in the Scripture passage, whether from an act in our past or in a current situation. Just like generations before us, we are living in the "last days." There is no way to change what is written, but you *can* change your life and help those around you to manifest godly attributes rather than the fallen nature of man. Use the wisdom in this Scripture to launch into your identity in Christ—it will change your life.

If we don't search for our identity in Him, we place our trust in ourselves. Confidence is built on what *we* do. More often than not, money is the driving force of identity for those who are lovers of self because money brings power. How quickly money can blur the boundaries of our ability to control what is right and wrong. When someone can freely spend money on selfish pleasures, the priority of a godly character is pushed away, but they can still look the part and play the game. Money can give people a false identity through the material things of the world instead of finding a true identity through the redeeming life of Christ. It is just as dangerous when people have little money because then they identify with their lack. With or without money, people tend to base identity on how much they do or do not have.

The tragedy of money is how quickly life becomes about "appearance." We go to church on Sunday to make the right appearance and to give out of our abundance, but there is no real power in our lives. The comfort of abundance drives us to complacency and we find that we are no longer lovers of God but lovers of our own pleasures. With the focus shifted to self, we lose insight to what is going on with others around us because we do not have time for anyone but ourselves. Once you venture down this path, it is not long before your life begins to bear fruit of the choices you have made, and they will ultimately expose you.

One of the key results of betrayal is exposure. Betrayal reveals who or what you trust. When the truth revealed shows that you have been trusting in self or material worth, it can be a very painful realization. The good news is that the damaging effects of betrayal can be used for your advantage when you allow the Holy Spirit to continue to build the character of God within you. Many times, betrayal prompts us to ask: what have we done wrong, or, how we have failed? Use the experience to penetrate deeper into relationship with Christ, as Paul admonishes in Scripture:

> *Test yourselves to see if you are in the faith: examine yourselves! Or do you not recognize this about yourselves, that Jesus Christ is in you—unless indeed you fail the test?* (2 Corinthians 13:5)

What is the test? The test is trust, and trust reveals identity. Is my trust firmly rooted in Christ or do I trust myself? Do I find my identity in Christ or is it connected to other people and things? Jeremiah clearly defined the end outcome of self-trust:

> *Cursed is the man who trusts in mankind and makes flesh his strength. And whose heart turns away from the Lord* (Jeremiah 17:5).

Our journey's quest must be driven by a desire to see the form of Christ manifested in us. We are searching for completeness, found by establishing God's heart, God's will, and God's place inside of our lives. The search is not about God blessing us for our works, rather it is about God dwelling in us and abiding with us. It is not about God blessing our character; it is about walking in His character. If betrayal in your life has pointed to the fact that you have failed the test, it has only exposed the issue that you trust self more than Him.

People are more educated today than ever before. It is easy to access information about any number of subjects through computers, technology, and electronic gadgets. You can even learn the latest news and events any time of day or night using cellular telephones, interactive television, and radio. Welcome to the future—the more you know, the more valuable you are. If you put your knowledge into an attractive package, you are that much farther ahead. The more we emphasize the importance of knowledge and information and keep packaging it with accolades of praise, the more we begin to trust in ourselves and our invincibility to any weakness.

Be informed, be educated, but do not forget that in our weakness Christ is made strong. Paul wrote to the Corinthians that recognizing weakness is a key element to becoming complete.

> *For we rejoice when we ourselves are weak but you are strong; this we also pray for, that you be made complete* (2 Corinthians 13:9).

We must be able to find the weakness in ourselves and then we can begin to apply faith. When I find my identity slipping and it seems that I cannot distinguish where or who I am, then I need to recognize that I have opened the door to satan. This is an area that has not been exposed to God and I need to go back and allow His character to come so that I can be made whole in Him.

To be "complete" is to have all the parts working together and/or to have all the necessary elements. You know that a creek bed will produce a smooth, polished stone because of the water flowing over the top of a rock. However, the part that is buried in the mud will still have many rough edges. In order for the rock to be polished on every side it would have to be turned over, exposing the side that was buried. Then the water would need to flow over this side to finish the transformation so that the entire rock was smooth and polished.

After the devastation of betrayal in my life, I would find myself staring at stones in the Brazos River in Texas. The stones were polished because of the constant flow of water that ran over them. I realized that the only way to smooth out the rough edges of my character and the weaknesses that had been exposed in the betrayal was to allow a constant, steady stream of intimacy to flow over me from the throne of God. To find completeness would require walking with integrity and maturity, upright before God and man. This is not a state that any of us can acquire by our own strength or determination. The only place to grow upright is face down at the Father's feet. When you allow the river of the love of God to flow freely over your open wounds, He begins to bind them up with an attitude of selflessness that Christ Himself carried.

THE WAY THAT SEEMS RIGHT

No one can tell you who you are. I have seen many leaders and ministers label the people who labor with them. Although a strong mentor or leader can help you realize your identity and provide godly counsel, you must find your own identity in the presence of God. Figuring out who you are happens over time and continues to change throughout your life. It is a daily walk, just like attaining an education. To be successful in your chosen profession, you must continue to learn the aspects of your trade and improve your skills. Change plays a critical role in remaining relevant and productive in your craft.

As you walk the path of discovering your identity, attitude will be molded in you. How you present yourself, how you carry on, and how you interact with others all comes from the paradigm of your identity. The Bible is very clear about the attitude we should carry:

> *Have this attitude in yourselves which was also in Christ Jesus, who, although He existed in the form of God did not regard equality with God a thing to be grasped, but emptied Himself, taking the form of a bond-servant, and being made in the likeness of men. Being found in appearance as a man, He humbled Himself by becoming obedient to the point of death even death on a cross* (Philippians 2:5-8).

Christ totally emptied Himself as a sacrifice, leaving His position of royalty to become a mere man so that we would have an example of the attitude we should have. When we truly find our identity in Christ, it will be evidenced by the humility that emanates from our attitude. If we are going to keep our identity in Him from slipping away and walk in the likeness of the Son of God, our lives should belong to the Father every day. In our walk with Christ, there are many struggles we face; it is not always easy to do the righteous thing, but it is the only way to continue to grow stronger in the identity God has given you.

Chapter 4

ENTANGLED WEB

Until you fully realize your true identity in Christ, life will be a constant search for the place where you "fit in." If you are secure in your identity, you will be more equipped to weather the storms of betrayal; if betrayal catches you in the middle of your search, you will quickly become ensnared.

Betrayal is comparable to a spider web, starting with one thread attaching to another. Soon more primary threads are spun, attaching to the first few, and the web begins to take shape. The spider slowly and precisely threads a fine net between the main strands using the gossamer, sticky silk that emits from its body. In a short while, though not complete, the web is strong enough to trap the spider's prey. The web abruptly halts unsuspecting insects as the wind propels them forward into a transparent and nearly invisible trap.

Once caught, the victim's reflex of struggles results in it becoming more entangled. Alerted by the movement, the spider quickly pounces and wraps it tightly in a cocoon. There is no escape, the insect dies in the silky fine threads and becomes food for the spider. The bigger the web, the stronger it seems. Any flying or crawling insect that ventures too close is doomed to become helplessly ensnared.

In the same way, betrayal begins as one person connects to another in relationship. Common characteristics tie the two together and soon there are numerous connecting points bracing the alliance, revealing any number of vulnerable access points. This is why betrayal is such an intimately agonizing experience—it touches us on a personal level. Once betrayal's web is woven, its purpose is to entangle you. The more you struggle, the more you fall prey to the purposes of the enemy for your demise. The complex web envelops you, diverting you from your destiny and purpose as your attention fixes on your own struggles and wounds. When you are trying to overcome the web in your own strength, you become just like the unsuspecting insect that ends up exhausted and lifeless.

The trials and experiences you pass through in life are there to take you to a greater platform, a greater glory. You have been purposed and destined for this lifetime and every step along the path is driving you toward fulfilling your specific purpose. Most often we remember this fact *after* we have exhausted ourselves in the struggle. Sometimes, we never realize it—we continue to look at the struggle as the end of all things and not as a revelation. Betrayal reveals the source of your trust. This is a fundamental truth you must remember when betrayal comes to your house.

Struggles Develop Discipline

When God begins to adjust our steps or take us from our current path to a new one that seems laden with web-wrought branches or uncertainty, we want to go in another direction. We do not see the value of the web. This is a good time to contemplate the promise in Hebrews:

> *You have not yet resisted to the point of shedding blood in your striving against sin; and you have forgotten the exhortation, which is addressed to you as sons: "My son, do not regard lightly the discipline of the Lord. Nor faint when you are reproved by Him; for those whom the Lord loves He disciplines, And He scourges every son whom He receives. It is for discipline that you endure; God deals with you as with sons; for what son is there whom his father does not discipline?"* (Hebrews 12:4-6)

God will direct and correct us in order to propel us toward the right place. Many times, one reason for the change in direction is for us to inspect our own hearts. Through the struggles, our personal nature and character is unveiled, revealing our true self. We see what we are and what our most basic responses are derived from as we walk through the process.

If you have ever disciplined a child, you have probably said, "This is for your own good and it hurts me more that it hurts you." Although a child rarely believes this statement at the time, it is true because we can see the entire spectrum of cause and effect. We know that if the child walks across the road in front of a speeding car it will kill him. So, we discipline to cause the child to look before crossing the road. Our discipline from the Father is for the same purpose. God wants us to hear Him before we take the steps. It does little good to ignore the voice of God, walk out into oncoming traffic and then say, "God bless what I have done." Discipline equips us to recognize and endure the struggle of the web. You just need the right perspective, as Scripture confirms:

> *All discipline for the moment seems not to be joyful, but sorrowful; yet to those who have been trained by it, afterwards it yields the peaceful fruit of righteousness. Therefore, strengthen the hands that are weak and the knees that are feeble, and make straight paths for your feet, so that the limb which is lame may not be put out of joint, but rather be healed* (Hebrews 12:11-13).

Life does not seem overly joyful when you are in the middle of a struggle, but God is focused on the outcome. Remember, to experience true fullness in your life, moments must be viewed from eternity's perspective. The Word says that discipline brings forth the peaceful fruit of righteousness. Going through the struggle strengthens you because it disciplines your senses. When you are disciplined you find out that your strength is actually birthed out of your weakness. You are able to recognize the need for the Father's strength.

When discipline manifests, its first touch on our lives seems to be painful or sorrowful. In reality, the development of discipline is simply a face-off of our natural ability against His supernatural ability. You might say that it is His way of changing our character to be more like His character. The apostle Paul was well accustomed to this type of fine-tuning.

> *Therefore I am well content with weaknesses, with insults, with distresses, with persecutions, with difficulties, for Christ's sake; for when I am weak, then I am strong* (2 Corinthians 12:10).

I have written at length about the positive effects of betrayal that come from having a reformed point of view regarding the experience—identity, discipline, strength from the Father, and so on. I do not want to diminish the struggle of betrayal. I know that it is as real as the breath you take, but when you grasp the full understanding that God is able and willing to guide you *through* the betrayal, you are more capable of dealing with it successfully. It is *His* righteousness that people will see in you after the discipline has had its perfecting work accomplished in your character. They will see in whom you have placed your trust and the level to which you have grown.

God's desire is that you place your feet on a straight course so that you are healed and made unconditionally and completely whole. To be made whole is to be in the likeness or image of God—no limitations, no boxes. His refining and disciplining process will enable you to walk upright as an example of Christ to others.

GOD'S EYES

Perception is a fundamental element of betrayal. The situation always depends on how you look at it. One time, a neighbor reported my wife's mother to the police. Minnie's mom, Laurnell, had sprayed weed killer along the fence line and it killed the neighbor's roses. The report came as quite a shock because this particular neighbor had enjoyed coffee and family dinners with Minnie's family on several different occasions. The ladies even shared a common gate between their homes so they could easily visit each other. Nevertheless, the accusation was made and the police report was filed without a word to Laurnell. Minnie's entire family felt betrayed and began to speak ill of the neighbor in defense of their mother.

Minnie's response was different, though. Rather than responding out of her own emotion, she exemplified the character of Christ while speaking to her mother one day. She spoke from the perspective of what Christ would do in the situation. This really touched Laurnell and she complimented her daughter on the fact that no matter what was said about someone or something, Minnie always saw the positive side. Viewing life through the eyes of the Father will most certainly change the way you look at and handle the events in your life.

This may seem like a very minor incident compared to the life-altering devastation that some families experience when it comes to betrayal, but any degree of betrayal has the potential to snatch you up into a web of destructive behavior. In order to show mercy toward her mother's neighbor, Minnie had to look through God's eyes rather than her own natural eyes. Minnie's choice of mercy impacted her mother far more than casting accusations ever could. Because she could tap into the character of Christ within her, Minnie was able to release the peace of God into this distressing situation.

The Word of God encourages us to pursue peace with all men so that we will not come short of the grace of God (see Hebrews 12:14-15). In all of my travels, I have never met a person who truly gets along with all people, all the time. Relating to and interacting with others are skills we must work at improving every day. In that regard, people act as tuning forks that work to point us toward a life of seeking after and trusting in God, refining His character within us. As we strive for peace with others, challenging situations can draw character flaws or bitterness to the surface and expose our humanity. If we exchange the flaws of our humanity for the grace of God, we will be empowered to walk through betrayal. If we hold on to our humanity, bitterness begins to stir up a whirlwind of trouble; we begin to trust in ourselves and fall short of God's grace.

GOD'S GRACE

The grace of God has been defined as His "unmerited favor," or something that we undeservingly receive because of His love for us. From my point of view, grace is more appropriately defined as "divine ability to function"—it is the Spirit of God within us that brings us into all truth. God's grace is the changing power that comes through the Holy Spirit as our lives begin to show His nature.

Through His death, Jesus' blood was placed on the mercy seat as the final sacrifice to hold back God's judgment. When Jesus returned to Heaven, He sent the Comforter, the Holy Spirit, to empower those who believe in Him (see John 16). Because of this, the Father sees only the blood of Christ (or His nature) when He looks at a believer. Earlier, we looked in-depth at how barren a life of works will leave you. Performing good deeds and giving money to your favorite charity are just as empty on their own merits. When we stand before the Father, He is looking for the character of His Son, not anything we have done in our own power. The Holy Spirit enables us to stand in the nature of Christ.

This is when our choice becomes apparent. We can choose to be identified through betrayal, or through Christ. If betrayal takes root, everything we touch with our hands loses its value. It becomes defiled because of the bitterness that starts to control all that we give to others.

Anytime you allow the root of betrayal to become bitter or corrupted, the good fruit in your life is ruined. Have you ever come across what looked like a perfectly ripe peach that almost made you recoil as you bit into it because of a dark, mealy bruise just under the surface? Betrayal takes on the same deception. It makes no difference how good you can make your actions or intentions look on the outside, the value and benefit of anything you have to offer is defiled because it originates out of a spirit of hurt and bitterness.

Esau is a man in Scripture who is controlled by bitterness. In an act of impatience, he sells his birthright because he is hungry. He trades his rightful inheritance as the first-born son for a bowl of soup. After his flesh is satisfied, he seeks to overcome with tears and sorrow but he finds no place of repentance. Betrayal takes root in his heart. Sadly, he did not count the cost of his bitterness and ends up nullifying the provisions of God for his life.

In times past, when I allowed betrayal to enter into my life and take root, bitterness and anger sprang up like wildfires, scorching everyone around me. My bitterness diverted the path God had placed before me. All of the provisions Christ had for my life went up in smoke. Ironically, each tiny fire started from a spark of offense. I did not slow down long enough to recognize the enemy's pattern of lies, deceit, and accusations. Instead, I ran with my perception of the situation and before long sparks of iniquity caught hold of the rubble in my heart and engulfed me.

Every part of my life changed for the worse because of the bitterness bottled up inside of me. The direction I was going in the ministry stopped completely and I started selling cars instead. I had lost my identity. I no longer knew who I was or whom I served, so I began to serve myself. It made sense to me at the time—people had wounded me, so I was going to wound them and others like them. It seemed like justice but I never stopped to consider the price. Thank God that through the challenge there were people around me who loved me with the love of the Father.

It was love that brought me to the realization that God was trying to create His character within me. He wanted me to see that I could not maneuver life in my own ability; I had to rely on His grace and ability. This was a difficult lesson to learn, especially when I realized that for all my crying about being betrayed, I was the one who had betrayed Him; yet He still loved me. The powerful love of God overcame the bitterness in my life. Only then was I able to experience the good that God had prepared for me.

Through the tool of betrayal in my life, I have learned that His love requires *response* and not *reaction*. If we react to a problem, we are working out of our own carnal ability and are not walking in the love of God. When we respond to a situation with the love of God, bitterness is cut short. This is the same way that the Father responded to the fall of man by sending His only begotten Son rather than reacting out of anger and destroying the world. He shows us repeatedly that *"love covers a multitude of sin."* We are quick to quote this verse over our own actions, but true love requires us to practice it with others as we walk through life (see 1 Peter 4:8).

Bitterness is a vicious captor. We can fall prey to it when we experience betrayal and we can also enslave others with it by releasing it toward them. This must stop. Jesus came to set every captive free. You do not have to be ensnared in the web of bitterness that comes from betrayal. It can be overcome through love that is born out of intimacy with the Father, which will in turn produce the grace of God in your life.

> *Therefore, since we have so great a cloud of witness surrounding us, let us also lay aside every encumbrance, and the sin which so easily entangles us, and let us run with endurance the race that is set before us, fixing our eyes on Jesus, the author and perfecter of faith, who for the joy set before Him endured the cross, despising the shame, and has sat down at the right hand of the throne of God. For consider Him who has endured such hostility by sinners against Himself, so that you may not grow weary and lose heart* (Hebrews 12:1-3).

You cannot lose focus. Millions who have gone before are cheering you on. Just remember that life is a race of endurance, not a series of short sprints. The only way to make it through the finish line is by finding your identity in Christ and overcoming the snare of the enemy's web. Jesus was able to find joy in all that He went through because His focus was fixed on the joy set before Him. He drew strength from an intimate relationship with the Father and that intimacy carried Him through every moment of pain, every strike of the whip. In the end, the Father was glorified in the Son and humanity was reunited with God.

At this juncture, I encourage you to contemplate the betrayals you have walked through in your own life. Intimacy with the Father is powerful enough to completely heal you and help you overcome all betrayal by the enemy. In order to be successful, you must first secure your identity in Jesus.

Chapter 5

WALKING IN YOUR IDENTITY

As pointed out previously, when you face betrayal it reveals who or what you trust, and you can either respond or react. If you are unsure of your identity in Christ when you face betrayal, you may become uncomfortable and overwhelmed with doubts and questions:

What did I do wrong?

Where did I fail?

Why is this happening to me?

What am I going to do now?

These are common questions we ask after we have been betrayed or even when we are in the midst of betrayal. Although it can be a painful, somewhat destructive experience, you can choose to look at this time as a starting point. Once your center of trust is exposed, you can begin to discover your identity. Identity will define in whom you trust.

It is not easy to see the formation of Christ's character being forged within you during this painful time, but it is this process that brings you to the place where you can trust the Father no matter what the challenge. Intimacy with Him will carry you through when position, fame, other people, and even your own strength leave you broken.

One of the keys to trusting in God is staying focused on Him and the direction He has given you—no matter what is going on around you. The struggle resulting from betrayal can be intense; either it will drive you deeper into relationship with the Father or it will cause you to start trusting yourself and your own abilities.

IDENTITY CRISIS

The Oxford American Dictionary defines *identity crisis* as "confusion in a person's mind." In other words, when you do not know who you are, you do not know who or what to trust. When you're not grounded in trusting God, you seem to face the same struggles over and over again—and each time, they take you by surprise. Just dealing with everyday issues can catch you off guard, isolating you more and more from Him. The issues of life deal with our nature or character, revealing those areas that can separate us from the nature of Christ. In First Peter 4:12, we are admonished to not be surprised at the trials that come to test us. Instead, we need to keep moving, press in further to God and keep rejoicing so that His glory will be made real in our lives.

Without the presence of God, escaping an identity crisis can be impossible. As a young man I had a hard time finding my identity. My father was not around and my mom worked all the time. My brother, Bob, was 11 years older than me and became a type of father figure for me. When I turned 8, my father came home from prison; then Bob got married, and moved out of the house. I felt so betrayed by Bob. I felt like he left me behind, that he did not love me anymore and that I must have done something wrong. I was not old enough to understand all of the dynamics of the situation. From my perspective, I was completely alone and I had no idea who I was.

My father was a man of few words with absolutely no tolerance for me. I did exactly as he said or I suffered his wrath. His idea of raising a child was to beat me as much as possible so I would be strong enough and mean enough to take on the same world he was raised in. In his eyes, I would either make something of myself through force or die trying. My earlier years of silently longing and crying out for a father's love were rewarded with terror and physical pain that left me feeling the sting of betrayal more sharply than the air passing through my battered lungs. This new reality solidified my perception that I was unloved and unwanted, nothing but a mistake from conception. My future was set on a course to play out just like my father's past—but worse, much worse.

My identity was built on the shattered remains of crushed hopes and past hurts. This type of identity will never allow you to reach beyond yourself to reach your destiny or potential. I realized this when I came to a point of divine intervention brought about by the fervent prayers of a mother's cry. At 26, I heard a new Voice speak to me. It seemed like a tiny stream of light came into my life at that moment and began to push back the shroud of darkness that had surrounded me. I heard God say, "Ron, I love you," and my life was changed. My world was turned upside down.

Within hours, my whole life began to make a U-turn. Somehow I had to grab a hold of the concept of trusting God rather than my own ability. Not only did I need to trust Him for myself, I had to trust God for my wife and daughter, my education, and the ministry God had written into my heart. For someone who had been so in control of every aspect of life, I realized that I was completely and utterly helpless without the guidance and direction of a genuine, loving Father. The dreams unleashed in my heart were too big to carry on my own and the cost of fulfilling those dreams was too far to stretch without the pliability of the Holy Spirit.

Renewed passion began to fuel the quest for my true identity in Christ. I trusted the Father with all that was most precious to me and He walked me through every stony path and stormy trial. Then, somewhere along the way, my trust in God began to bow to the acceptance of man. I stopped trusting God, who had brought me out of the mire and placed my feet on solid ground. I had become secure in my identity in Christ, and without realizing it I began to grow comfortable in that success, as if I was the one who had made it come about. Slowly my thoughts began to originate from my own knowledge of the world and how to take care of issues. I knew that *I* could do it. Does this sound familiar?

While walking along, somewhere the path veered ever so slightly and my unshakable trust in the Father, who called me and restored me, shifted to a trust in my own strengths and abilities. I still felt close to God. I still felt that I was following His call and doing His will, but I was positioning myself for a fall without even realizing it. My identity became the ministry I had built. Believe me, the moment you begin to think you are more than you are, you have set yourself up with a false identity, and betrayal is on its way to your door, because the birthplace of betrayal is presumption.

As time went by and the ministry grew, the people closest to me betrayed me. As I wrote in Chapter One their betrayal caused the downfall of all that I was. All that I had and everything that had been accomplished through my life came crashing down around me. I had skillfully learned to trust me, myself, and I—I could handle anything; until I saw firsthand just how fragile a foundation built on self is.

I did not grasp the message God was giving me:

> ...*do not be surprised at the fiery ordeal among you which comes upon you for your testing*...(1 Peter 4:12).

When the test came to me, testing who I trusted, I failed and it was devastating. The betrayal in my life shouted out the source of my trust—me. When you place your trust in yourself, you lay out the welcome mat for your adversary. Through his nature, the king of self-promotion, satan, knows just how to take you down piece by piece.

> *Be of sober spirit, be on the alert. Your adversary, the devil, prowls around like a roaring lion, seeking someone to devour* (1 Peter 5:8).

Betrayal began to take its root in me and I completely lost my identity. I was being devoured in large bites that took me almost to my death. My faith rested in my own strength, in the ministry I thought was mine—and it was all a lie. I had become the very icon that I had hated as a non-Christian; I was just like those who had turned my stomach concerning the things of God. Under the heavy weight of religion, power, and pride, I bowed low enough to be reminded that my strength could never carry me through. Then, once again, in the stillness of brokenness, I heard the Father: "Ron, I love you. Do you love me?" The God of grace had shown up at my weakest point to strengthen and establish me.

But resist him, firm in your faith, knowing that the same experiences of suffering are being accomplished by your brethren who are in the world. After you have suffered for a little while, the God of all grace, who called you to His eternal glory in Christ, will Himself perfect, confirm, strengthen and establish you (1 Peter 5:9-10).

Now I am still in the process, but the struggle does not catch me unaware. Even as I write this portion of the book, I am sitting in a small town parking lot in a broken down vehicle waiting for a special belt that had to be ordered. I am not even close to my destination and now I have been delayed for several days. I am sure that you can relate to glitches while walking along the journey. The difference for me now is that I have the peace of God—despite the delay, despite the hassle. I know the root of my trust. Will I have more struggles along the journey? Absolutely. Will I always be able to face each trial with a calm sense of assurance and trust in my Father? I really cannot say, but I know that today I did. That means I have something to draw from the next time hardship comes, and believe me, there will be a next time.

We cannot allow the circumstances of life to identify us or take away from our identity in Christ. Sometimes calamity comes upon us so that we can see in whom we trust. God knows exactly where we are but He wants us to know our purpose in life. It is good for us to see Him at work in our lives and experience His deliverance firsthand. God intimately knows who we are, where we are in Him, and what we will accomplish. There are times we may think we know exactly who we are and what we are doing but when the test comes, we find out that we do not have a clue. I cannot stress this point enough—the struggles of life help you remember that the reality of what you are is only what God is in you. Everything else is dust. This is a walk of faith and intimacy. The strength that carries you to the end of the adventure is realizing that your value is based on the essence of God's presence in your life and walking in His presence by faith.

A Test of Character

Appropriating faith is the first step to building a solid foundation on Christ and realizing your true identity. Some will tell you that if you are going through struggles, it is because you are out of faith or that you have failed. According to the Word, this is not true. In fact, from my experience, I believe that if you have not gone through tests or trials then you have never met God. This may seem like a bold statement, but the reality of Christ's love is that we are put in the test of life to reveal our character.

A very good friend of mine told me that *God will offend your mind to reveal your heart.* God will put you in situations to reveal your character. As long as you walk with Him, He will continually deal with the human nature inside of you in an effort to define and refine the nature of Christ.

There are times in my life when I feel like I am being pulled through a knothole backward. I make it, but before I can pick myself up, I am flying right back through. Around the bend, I find myself back in the same place being pulled through again, but instead of the hole becoming larger as I hurl through the cramped opening, it becomes smaller and smaller each time. The knothole becomes smaller because God wants more of my character shaved away so that His nature will be manifested in me. Every time a part of my fallen nature is skimmed away, more of God's nature can be refined within me. Although the knothole is not a comfortable experience, it is my desire that one day the hole will be so small that it eliminates my carnal will. Then, when I face the Father for judgment it will be His Son that He sees.

Scripture admonishes us that to the degree we share in the suffering of Christ, we should keep on rejoicing. Christ learned obedience through suffering as a human. In the end, He was willing to obey His Father to His own shame and death. Because He understood that the will of God leads us to our destiny and purpose, no suffering was greater than that joy set before Him. His life was and is in the Father. His identity was in His destiny.

The purpose of your suffering today is learning how to overcome the struggle through faith in God, realizing that He is glorified when you overcome. The enemy brings betrayal into your life so you will identify with the failure and the struggle. Do not let that struggle or suffering control or manipulate you any longer. As you walk through betrayal, God will show you and the world who you really are if you will stay focused on Him. Then you can rejoice with great enthusiasm because you know that God is working His character within you.

The road to living a successful life and overcoming betrayal is in rejoicing through the struggle as His nature is established within you. In the face of betrayal, you must remember that you are not a failure. You have not missed out on God by taking a particular path. Your struggle is a tool to produce Christ's character. When His joy and peace rule in every situation of your life, the revelation of His glory is revealed not only to you but to everyone around you as well. You are an example of God's work and your life will reveal His goodness.

Keep in mind that betrayal is always in the eyes of the beholder. We all see betrayal from our own point of view. Sometimes people are not out to betray us, they simply believe that they are helping us to become a better person. They think we need to change in order for God to work the works of righteousness within us. Who do I trust? This is the question you should always ask. Your destiny is in the hand of God. When this is settled in your heart, peace enters and confirms that all things work to the good of those who love the Lord and are called according to His purpose. True peace comes from God—not people, money, or power. He knows right where you are and exactly what you need to fulfill your purpose.

If we are going to fully walk as people of purpose, we must be able to hear God's voice just as clearly as Christ heard the Father. Having intimate communication with the Father fueled Christ's devotion to carry out the Father's plan. Ironically, the place at the Father's feet where Christ spent most of His time is where we spend the least amount of time. Jesus separated Himself from others to pray and He listened to what the Father had to say. In the course of an average day, if we pray for our food we feel good about it. If we spend time in church praying, we think that will be good for about a week. We shouldn't wonder, then, why we are so feeble against the attacks of the enemy when we spend so little time communicating with God the Father.

When Moses led the people from the Red Sea to the desert the people began to grumble. They were in a struggle—the water was bitter and they were thirsty. Moses cried out to God and the Lord showed him a tree that he could throw into the water so that it would become sweet and drinkable. This was a test from God—the purpose was to recognize and give heed to the voice of the Lord (see Exodus 15:25-26).

Even after God provided the water, the children of Israel went into another time of struggle and began to grumble again. They had received water but now they were hungry. Again, God provided for them so that they would know that it was the Lord God who brought them out of Egypt. Still they complained that they would have been better off to have died in captivity than to be inconvenienced in a wilderness (see Exodus 16-17).

We are not so different today. We do not like to be unhappy or inconvenienced. If life starts becoming too uncomfortable as a believer, we must be out of God's will. We start grumbling against whatever is causing the betrayal instead of going to God to hear His voice on the matter. Moses went to God on behalf of the children of Israel because He knew God's *ways*—the people could only identify with God's *acts*. When we live a life of religion or church, we become accustomed to God's acts. It is time to go beyond the surface into intimacy so that we can truly learn the Father's ways.

Your character will be tested. If you yield your heart to God, listen to what is spoken, and do right, many things will be accomplished in your character. God will make provision for you; He will free you from the curse so you can live in His covenant blessings. He will direct the path of the righteous.

THE PURPOSE OF THE STRUGGLE

For a believer, betrayal is a teacher, strengthener, revealer, and helper. Non-believers experience betrayal as well, but do not have an answer to the struggle. In this situation, they are consumed with a full blown identity crises because they cannot draw purpose out of the struggle. This feeling of helplessness drives many people to take emotion-dulling prescription drugs or to turn to dangerous lifestyles in an effort to find some semblance of peace. Others who have felt the sting of betrayal fill up psychiatrist appointment books because they have so many questions plaguing them through restless nights, tormenting them relentlessly—why don't people like me, why is my job so hard, why can't my son behave, why do I have no peace?

According to society, psychiatrists are supposed to be the experts. They are educated, well trained, and skilled at helping people find inner peace. Still, the best that most psychiatrists provide is simply a sounding board for people to talk to. Although they cannot solve your problem, they make sure that you understand that you cannot overcome your problem on your own. So, you talk through your struggles in the search to find answers. The problem is that you can talk for years without ever uncovering the root of your identity crisis. In this type of setting, you deal only with the moment or the issues on the surface but the root stays buried and can cause symptoms to resurface for years. The cycle of betrayal will continue in our lives until you allow Christ to reveal the root.

When the children of Israel complained against Moses, they perceived that he had betrayed them and had led them to their death, when in fact they were on the road to freedom and abundance. Betrayal is always in the eyes of the perceiver. One person will see a situation a certain way, another will see it completely different. Each of us can be deceived by our perception versus reality. It is easy to start complaining and grumbling against another individual when we feel betrayed. We are looking for someone to blame. Sometimes, without intimacy, we even blame God. We question how a loving God could allow us to experience such pain rather than seeing the struggle as a passage to an intimate relationship with our Redeemer.

There are days when I act just like the people described in Exodus. I would rather die in Egypt with the perception of no trials or pain than die from hunger in the desert where my Deliverer nourishes me from His hand—all because the cost of the struggle seems too great. What is in your heart? Solomon, the wisest man who ever lived, challenges us to go beyond ourselves.

Trust in the Lord with all your heart, And do not lean on your own understanding. In all your ways acknowledge Him, And he will make your paths straight (Proverbs 3:5-6).

Without intimacy with the Father, our perceptions will always be based out of our carnal mind, focused on the moment rather than on eternity. We will lock ourselves into a cycle where we can never become anything greater than our own abilities will allow because we stay tied to the smallness of humanity rather than the greatness of our God. *Whatever you are intimate with, you will be passionate about.* If there is no intimacy in your life with the presence of God, there will be no provision of God that you can see. Provision is one way in which God manifests His glory. It is how He shows you that He loves you and cares about you; it displays that He is the true and living God who delivers you from bondage.

Struggles can drive you toward intimacy with the Father. Intimacy develops trust; . Trust that Christ will not only provide for you but He will also lead you through the hardship. In order to survive the test and walk in our God-given identity, we must have confidence that God is who He says He is and that what He says, He will do. He is not only our Creator, but He is also the author and finisher of our faith, the God who establishes His domain through us. The test of life comes to each of us, so we will show our love for Him and experience His love for us.

Chapter 6

TIED TO THE POST

Recognizing who you are in Christ and maturing to the point of walking in that persona is the absolute best thing you can do for yourself *and* for those you love. When you know who you are, you have the ability to quickly move past trivial matters that can easily sidetrack someone who is battling a low confidence level identity crisis. Armed with a sense of purpose and destiny, you are ready to charge forward and accomplish great things. I felt exactly this way when Jesus saved me. I knew that no matter what God asked me to do, I could do it because of His greatness. Contagious optimism fuels the excitement of unknown possibilities in your life. This is the stage where the true test of maturity begins.

Maybe you have been in the struggle—you have felt broken, beaten, and at the breaking point—then you were washed in the warm Balm of Gilead that mended your wounds. Maybe you have just finally figured out who you are and stopped living in the shadow of other people. Either way, you are tied to the post, or starting point, ready to begin a new journey.

This is where we see the colt in Matthew 21. Just imagine for a few moments that you are that colt. You have been standing quietly next to your mom, intently watching everything that is going on. There is an unexplainable excitement in the air; you want to move about and play, embracing the energy of the moment but you can't because you are securely tied to the post.

Soon, some strangers come and untie you and your mom and begin to lead you away from your post. You are so excited that you are finally able to do something else besides standing still and waiting—watching as life passes you by. From the corner of your eye, you see your master just watching as the men lead you both away. Inside of you there is a feeling that can't be defined, a strange combination of adventure and elation. Something fantastic is lying just beyond your grasp of understanding.

Suddenly, the small entourage stops and the men begin to lay robes on your back. A man sits down on top of the robes. You feel every fiber of the soft, lavish garments and the weight of the man presses into your backbone. It is still hard to understand that you are the one chosen rather than your mom. Destiny inside tells you that this is your defining moment. As you begin to parade into the city, more robes and cloaks are placed on the road in front of you. Some people are even making a carpet of palm branches for you to walk upon.

All around you, people are clapping and raising their hands. The air is charged with electric excitement. The crowd is triumphantly shouting, "Hosanna in the highest, blessed is He who comes in the name of the Lord." The man who you are carrying is being celebrated in the streets of Jerusalem. Out of all the colts and horses in the land, you have been chosen. How special you feel! Your mom never had a reception of branches placed before her or held such a notable man on her back. This must be your breakthrough into greatness. Things will definitely be different now.

OUT OF THE SPOTLIGHT

Before you know it, you have reached the end of the road. The man slips down off your back. Surely He will keep you beside Him because of the important moment you have just shared. To your dismay, you are returned to the post, retied, and left behind. You are right back where you started. If you could only have a few more minutes, you could show the strangers how valuable you are, how much you could do for them. The post is quiet and boring—you do not want to stay there. You want to run free and carry the important man down another street in another city. You want to feel the plush blanket as it warms your backbone and hear the crunch of the palm branches underfoot again. But here you are, tied with just enough rope to bend your head and nibble at the tuft of grass near your feet, and silence is the only blanket that covers you.

This is how we feel sometimes when we begin to truly walk in the identity God has planned for us. We begin to move down a path of greatness and excitement. People start to pay attention to what we have to say and what we are doing. Then, too quickly, the spotlight shuts down like in an abandoned theater house and we are back at the starting point where everything is calm. We are all alone and there is only silence.

There have been so many times when I felt the anointing powerfully on my life. The presence of God was being revealed in and through me in new and dynamic ways. The ministry was booming and people surrounded me. The roar of the crowd was nearly deafening, creating a momentum in my spirit that propelled me forward into more adventures. Then, all of a sudden, I would find myself tied to the post in a place of waiting. Nothing was happening, there were no more crowds cheering or clapping and there were no royal robes upon my back.

Be careful that you do not lose that which you have obtained when you find yourself staring at the post. You see, the power of this post is that it can be a launching-pad or it can become a post of betrayal. You walk through a great situation and when that situation comes to a close you are given the opportunity to prove your maturity or your uncertainty. If you do not accept the place of waiting, you begin to lose your identity and perceive that you have been betrayed. You think that all that was once great in your life has been snatched from you. Betrayal in a person's life comes when reality sets in beyond the anointing or beyond the moment, but the moment can only be manifested by preparation.

In the silence at the post, you begin to reason that people do not love you after all. The longer you stay there, the more you begin to feel as if you did something wrong when you were away from the post and now you are being punished by having to stand there. Entertaining this pattern of thought leads you to believe that you have failed and you are finished. Now the door is wide open for the enemy to usher in self-induced rejection born out of doubt. Rejection tells us that we are tied to the post because no one wants us, we have been betrayed, and all that is great within us will be stripped bare, never to be used of God again.

This may seem a bit dramatic, but the truth is that our carnal nature pulls us down to a place of broken humanity. Part of the reason we are tied to the post is to bring about maturity. The maturing process is learning the ability to press on in spite of circumstances—because we are tied to something greater. It is only the Spirit of God that allows us to go above and beyond the moment and realize who we are regardless of what acts we are performing, regardless of what words we are speaking, and regardless of who is listening.

POST OF PREPARATION

Although we feel as if we are tied to a post of rejection, in truth we are tied to a post of preparation. Remember, Jesus knew exactly where the donkey and colt were waiting. He knew that they were prepared for Him. That is why He could tell the disciples to go and get the animals, telling anyone who questioned them that the Master had sent them (see Matthew 21:2-3).

When we experience the struggle of betrayal, we find ourselves tied to a post. The natural response is to pull against the rope that holds us to the post because we cannot find the reason for being there. We are looking only at the moment rather than at our destiny. The post is where God prepares you for your next move. Being able to wait at the post is an act of maturing in Christ.

If you have ever been around true cowboys and the horses that they ride, you will notice a remarkable relationship between the horse and rider. Horses spend a great deal of time tied to the fence, standing and waiting for the rider. They know that the ordeal before them may take all that they have; it may even take a bit more. Still, they are willing to wait because they have been trained in their task and they trust the rider.

God is preparing each of us for the task He has created for our lives from the foundation of time. When He establishes the groundwork we need, we are given the direction to go forward to the next level. Then He brings us back to the post and prepares us for an even greater move. Our human nature makes it hard for us to understand this process. We want to hold on to the abilities we have mastered or the great feats we have accomplished. Once we have been a part of something great, it is almost impossible to go back and receive more training because we think we know all that there is to know.

The problem is that when we reject the training of God, we find ourselves circling the same mountain again and again. God does not want this, but if we continue to pull against the rope and refuse to listen, He will bring us to the place where we are forcibly tied to the post. We are there for a reason. Just like there will always be valleys and peaks in life, maturity enables us to stop viewing the easy times as the "peaks" and the struggles as "valleys." God uses the entire process to move us toward the fulfillment of our destiny. We are built as His dwelling place, line upon line, precept upon precept, and from one glory to the next.

Our identity must be secure in spite of what we feel or what we are experiencing. Sometimes when God uses us mightily, it is very easy to draw our identity from His presence on our lives, from the acceptance of people, or from what we are doing. Keeping our hearts locked in that place will ultimately lead to a feeling of betrayal. God is moving us forward. When God wants to transition us from one place to another, we must be willing to go back to the post of preparation—the post of intimacy. We have to go back home to the place where we began.

It may feel like moving back to the post is taking a huge step backward when, in reality, it is launching you forward. This is a point you must understand. I do not believe in going backward. I have learned many valuable lessons from my past, but it does not define me. I have no need to go back in my life and dwell on the events that have happened. The old man has died and no longer lives within me. My focus is on receiving the training God has for me *today* so that I will be ready for the next move, no matter what that move looks like. The post is where intimacy with the Father is refined and seared into my heart so that my next move is always right in step with His plan for me. More often than not, intimacy and preparation in my life is accomplished through my perception of betrayal.

My family and I used to live on a ranch in Texas. We had several horses and there was one horse in particular that was always difficult to load into the trailer. She was skittish and pulled hard against the reigns. Nothing I did would break her of this reaction. I found out that when she was being trained to go into a trailer, the owner would jerk down on the reigns and try to force her up into the trailer. She became accustomed to resisting because she was unsure about what was happening. This is the same reaction people have when someone tries to get us to go in a direction we are not sure of—we resist. As a result, when God begins to pull the reigns and secure us to the post of preparation, we have a hard time separating His desire to train and equip us from the control and manipulation we have felt from others.

To some degree, we have all experienced someone trying to force his or her own agenda in our lives and we become somewhat guarded. When God desires to build us up at the post, the pressure begins to pull us this way or that and we dig in our heels and stand our ground, pulling hard against the rope. Whether someone else is pulling you away from the tugging of God or you are pulling away yourself, *if you do not see beyond the moment, the moment will begin to identify you.* The struggle begins to deceitfully declare that you have missed God and failed. You are mocked by the fact that you once walked in His glory and anointing, were welcomed by all, and now that is gone and you are nothing.

SEEING BEYOND THE MOMENT

Now that I understand that being tied to the post is a place to prepare me to go to the next level, I am relaxed just like the horse patiently waiting for the rider to take his stance. I realize that the post is where God readies me for a shift—generally a complete paradigm shift. A *paradigm* is an example or model of how something should be done. God desires to use each of us, in our designed place of influence, as models to show others how things should be done. This mindset originates from the truth that the good example in my life is not me, but it is Christ who lives in me. God may never repeat the marvelous acts He has done in and through my life, yet I know that He will continually move me to a greater place if I will set my eyes on that which is above instead of that which is behind.

The post is a place where our character or attributes are clearly exposed so that we can deal with them according to the grace of God. The life of Paul is a strong example of how God can change a man who is focused on Him; still, the change was a progression that Paul had to embrace. As Saul, he had murdered the disciples of the Lord and zealously fought against the uprising of Christianity resulting from Christ's death and resurrection. In a divine encounter on the road to Damascus, Saul came face to face with the God he had been betraying. In one Bible translation, Jesus says to Saul, "Why are you kicking against the pricks?" Saul fought against the very elements that would give him life. He defiled the instrument that could bring him to his purpose and destiny. When deception was stripped away from Saul's life, he allowed God to take him through the transformation of becoming Paul, the writer of over half of the New Testament (see Acts 9).

The post of preparation can be seen in many different ways. So many times we want to fight the post. We cry out to God asking how, why, and how much longer will we have to endure. We never consider that the Lord is trying to get our attention because we are so busy and caught up in our own lives, or even doing what we believe is His work, that we have lost sight of Him. Even though our actions are born out of our own ideas and abilities, we ask God to bless them rather than seeking God first for His blessing and direction and then doing what He commands.

Jesus told Saul that He had been trying to get his attention but Saul kept fighting Him. This is a man who had been trained in the Scriptures and educated in the matters of God, yet somehow he did not recognize Truth until he was stopped cold. It is clear that Saul betrayed Christ and persecuted believers, but he also passionately believed that he was serving God through his actions. Naturally, when he experienced resistance, he began to kick against the pricks, fighting for his own perspective.

Along your journey, there will be times when the Lord is working through you and you feel that because of this you are shielded. Still, somehow you find yourself betrayed by a situation and you begin to question why you had to experience it. You begin to fight and resist, struggling to overcome this great obstacle. The key is in stopping long enough to search out the Father's heart and hear His perspective on what is going on in your life. Maybe you are kicking against His refining pricks that have been placed in your path to cause you to go to the next level—like Paul.

There were times when situations were placed along my path that seemed to be betrayals because I did not see what God was doing in my life. I began to take the assaults personally and found myself blinded, just like Paul. It is in this blinded state where God unveils His light. Right in the middle of kicking and screaming against the corrective embrace of God, I began to hear Jesus speak to my destiny and purpose just as I imagine He spoke to Paul.

When we look at betrayal as an enemy instead of a refining tool of God in our lives, it looks like we have reached a hopeless dead end. I challenge you to realize that it is actually the beginning of a great new paradigm that the Father wants to unveil within your spirit.

SEEKING GOD

How many times have you found yourself in the midst of a change or transition that caused you to fast and pray? It seems that questioning and doubt are normal reactions to a shift in our lives. We become introspective and begin reviewing our actions, our decisions, and the paths we have taken through life. The wonder of fasting is that it brings us to the place where we can more clearly hear the voice of the Father. Prayer and fasting enables us to become more intimate with God, fine-tuning our hearing so that our ears are receptive to the soft, still voice of our Maker.

Fasting allows us to unleash our spirit to have full reign over our human nature. In this place of order, the fighting and pulling against the pricks comes to a stop. Our questioning and wild reasoning is silenced and our inquisitive intellect bows to the divine wisdom of the Father. Life focuses on hearing His voice and following His direction. Out of our spirit, we connect to the Spirit of God and cry, "Father, you must tell me. You must speak and lead my steps." Now we have arrived. The only place to start is right where we are and the first step always originates at the feet of the Father.

This is a familiar Scripture to lean on while seeking God: *"unless the Lord builds the house, the laborers labor in vain"* (see Psalm 127:1). When you find yourself at the point where you are laboring, and no matter how hard you labor nothing is accomplished, then you are working out of your own strength. You are not relying on the strength of God and everything you do will be in vain until you stop and seek Him. The most essential need in my life is my need for God. I must walk in relationship with Him and commune with Him. I have to know the Father. Unless He reveals Himself to me, everything that I do in His name will be in vain.

If the price of pursuing intimacy with the Father is persecution by the enemy, then the Lord will equip me with the grace to stand through that persecution. When I have intimacy, I am able to look beyond the struggle back to the heart of Jesus and pull from the same strength and authority that enabled Him to walk through the most extreme betrayal. Because I know that the Father does everything for my good I will not focus on the betrayal; instead I will be asking, "What should I learn from this? Where do You want me to go? What do You want me to accomplish?" The pleading of my heart falls upon the altar, "Lord, cleanse me and use me for Your Kingdom—whatever the cost."

Chapter 7

EMBRACING THE POST

No account in the Bible gives a clearer depiction of a life of struggles, betrayal, and miraculous transformation than the life of Paul. After Paul's encounter with a holy and loving God, he became a man of altered passion. As he began to preach in the streets of Damascus, people were stirred up because they identified him with his past acts. When he had originally begun his journey to Damascus, Paul's intent was to persecute believers. Upon arrival at his destination, he was a changed man—a man of God. Consequently, he became the object of persecution by the religious Hellenistic Jews, so much so that he had to flee for his life in the middle of the night (see Acts 9).

Unfortunately, the welcome into Jerusalem was not much better. The disciples did not believe that Paul had changed and regarded him with open skepticism. His words were truth, but the zealous actions of this infamous Pharisee could not be easily dismissed. How quickly we can forget that without the Father's outstretched arm of mercy, we would all surely die. However, it was death—death to himself—that transformed Saul to Paul. In that state of fragile vulnerability, God reached into his soul and changed his life. I can imagine that as Paul was quickened by the breath of God, he heard the Father whisper, "Your past does not define your destiny, my son," because he never looked back.

Your Past Does Not Define Your Destiny

Paul's encounter with God prepared him to run the race he had been destined for. From the moment he stood up on the Damascus Road, a new type of persecution was waiting to enter his life. In his temporary blindness, Paul learned that being a disciple of Christ required a different process, a deeper dimension than anything he had previously known. The secret to delving deeper into God and growing stronger is the same for us today as it was for Paul—stop kicking against the pricks and embrace the post. It is here where the voice of your spirit cries out, "Father, have your way in my life, no matter what it takes to accomplish my destiny and the purpose for which you have sent me to the earth."

God was able to move through Paul powerfully by many acts and wonders because Paul understood how to discern the moving and direction of God. He had been taught at the post and became intimate with the teacher. Because of intimate revelation, he was willing to pay the price to be used by God. He became a renowned mouthpiece for the Father at great consequence to himself. Yet, he declares that the price he paid did not compare to the reward he knew was in front of him (see 2 Cor. 11:21–12:6).

Paul's outspoken zeal centered him in the middle of many disputes with Barnabas, Peter, and others. At any time, he could have considered their actions as betrayal as he pushed through the rejection of his peers time and time again. He knew the truth that we today must cling to if we are to overcome betrayal in our lives: to walk in the purposes and destiny of God is to walk in a continual paradigm shift. We must be open to a continually changing mindset concerning the matters of God.

Churches, small businesses, corporations, and community groups all address their viewpoints on how we should react to change. With a plethora of self-help tools at our fingertips, we tend to look at the things we are going through as a disturbance. When everything is going great, people are excited about what is happening. As soon as a challenge confronts us that seems to be taking us in the wrong direction, we begin a meltdown. We need to stop and consider that the Spirit of God is trying to lead us through a change of character and that we are pulling against Him. It may come in the form of another person, our job, or even a family member trying to present a different point of view. Look beyond the struggle and see the reward of greater intimacy with the Father.

Post of Rejection

In the previous chapter, I wrote in depth about the preparation that takes place when we are tied to the post. We grow and mature by working through feelings of rejection and self-doubt that dissolve into revelation and intimacy. There are times when God draws us back to the post through the natural timing of an event that has run its course and we feel a release drawing us to the next level. There are also times when the betrayal of others drives us back to the post and it becomes a post of rejection inflicted by people.

The process of betrayal brings about feelings of rejection. Though rejection is a natural emotion of life, it is powerful enough to knock you completely off course if you are caught unaware. People will reject you because of your faith, because of what God has done in your life, because of your principles, even because of the destiny or giftings in your life. Why wouldn't the Father take these cruel situations away from us and shelter us under His wing? We *are* sheltered—sheltered by the post where we will be quiet and still, allowing God to work His character through us as He works out the pain. By dealing with rejection, betrayal becomes an exacting process to establish not only your destiny and purpose on the earth, but also to reveal in whom you trust.

Paul had spent time at the post of preparation where God laid out the blueprint of the Kingdom upon his heart. Because of this, Paul could go back to the post even when it was covered with rejection and glean the learning points that strengthened him to return to the crowds and minister truth. Something happens at the post of rejection. The pain and isolation drive you to a place of silence where you hear the Father and begin to walk with the Son. Godly attributes are skillfully crafted into you as you walk through betrayal and rejection. You become pure by your relationship and intimacy with God. Then, as with Paul, personal intimacy with the Father will cause you to plead with others and draw them unto Christ as you manifest the heart of God. We see this in Paul's relationship with the church at Corinth:

> *Therefore I urge you, brethren, by the mercies of God, to present your bodies a living and holy sacrifice, acceptable to God, which is your spiritual service of worship. And do not be conformed to this world, but be transformed by the renewing of your mind, that you may prove what the will of God is, that which is good and acceptable and perfect. For through the grace given to me I say to everyone among you not to think more highly of himself than he ought to think; but to think so as to have*

sound judgment, as God has allotted to each a measure of faith (Romans 12:1-3).

I fear that some of the intellectual and technological advancements of today have made things more complicated. At times, even the "simplicity" of modern day computers can make an average day frustrating and challenging—especially for me! But our walk with God should be simple and pure. Our lives are to be presented as a living and holy sacrifice unto Him—willingly. Whenever we find ourselves laboring to do what is right, it means we are walking in our own ability.

Many people who are standing at the post are pulling against it. They are fighting burnout, stress, anxiety, or loneliness. They have lost the simple power of the Word of God to help them. This is what happens when you try to overcome betrayal or rejection in your own strength or reasoning. Stop and be still. Renew your mind by reading, studying, and absorbing the Word of God—but do not memorize only the law. Laws impose burdens and walking explicitly by the law will cause you to struggle in your relationship with God (see Matthew 5:17). If you obey rules without understanding the character of God, you will miss the intimacy of the Father's heart, His presence, and the power of His Spirit.

As we travel across this country and around the world, my heart breaks when I see so many people wasting time on this precious journey because they are consumed by struggles and hurt. They have strayed off of the path of simplicity and farther away from seeing that God's will is good, acceptable, and perfect.

When betrayal comes into our lives and we begin to experience rejection, God is dealing with the motive and intent of our heart. He is testing the purity of our motives to make sure they are undefiled by the accolades of people. This is to safeguard us.

If we are swayed by human motivation, we are an easy target for repeated attacks of rejection. This process at the post will bring us to purity of devotion to Christ. We must learn how to leave the pain at the post or we will never continue the journey. If we don't continue the journey, we will not inherit the dream or vision of God for our lives and destiny will remain unfulfilled.

Enjoy the Journey

Inherit the Dream

Fulfill Your Destiny

When you find your identity in God, your perception of betrayal will be different. A relationship with Christ is the very essence of life. Intimacy with the Lord will give you a passion for His ways. Passion is the driving force to walk through betrayal, to make it to the other side. Allow your mind to be transformed and find the plan and purpose of God in your life.

WILLING TO CHANGE

Have you ever wanted to change anything in your life? Of course you have. At one time or another, I imagine that each of us has wanted to change something about our physical appearance, our position in life, our job, or our homes. Change affects every area of our lives. What is the defining difference between two people who have prepared for a marathon when only one finishes the race? Focus. Jesus stated that He endured the Cross because of the prize set before Him. We are in the endurance race of a lifetime. If we cannot focus our minds and hearts on the ultimate goal of being with Him, then during the changes that occur, we will not have the strength to endure the death of our flesh.

There have been powerful outpourings of God throughout the years. Many movements of God have occurred even in my lifetime. When we see these outpourings of His presence, we have to choose whether or not to embrace the change or resist it and cling to the past. I realized that if I did not move with the Father I could only teach what He had done in the past and not what is happening now. Ultimately, this would result in dead, stale teachings that God no longer breathed on. We must be discerning and willing to move when renewal breaks out or a movement of God takes place. Whenever God makes a shift in the heavens, it affects the earth and requires a response. Changing to be in step with Jesus will keep us focused on our purpose.

In the midst of change, there is a steadiness. We know that *"Jesus Christ is the same yesterday and today forever"* (Heb. 13:8). Even with change swarming around us, the principles and truth of God remain constant—only people and circumstances change. Christ is called the Rock because He is solid (see 1 Corinthians 1:4). Some changes make it seem like the sand is shifting dangerously all around us, as well as in us. But the shifting works to change us so we will represent the Solid Rock. We exhibit the continual evolving of the Kingdom of God—the Kingdom that is within us—which must continually be manifested in greater dimensions as we grow in Christ.

As a church leader, if you refuse to experience the renewal or transition brought about by the current moving of God, you will stop growing and teach only from the last paradigm you accepted. I believe this is how many Bible colleges were established. Leaders began to teach what God had done for them based on past experience and because they were unwilling to move again the teachings have become stagnant. It is easy to become comfortable, especially when the aspect of changing is covered by challenges that will require you to stretch beyond yourself. Every time, you move forward through a transition, your church or ministry is directly effected by the change. The struggle that is set before you is the testing of your faith. You will grow stronger as a result of accepting change. Will you settle for being comfortable or accept the challenge to grow?

I thank God for the generations that have gone before, enabling us to be where we are today. But if we do not learn that every transition has been a preparation for the next move, we will fall short of all that God has for us and we will fail the next generation. When Jesus said that we would do greater things in the last days, He was referring to change. Embracing change will bring about a greater manifestation of the presence of God and a greater revelation of the purpose of the Father's Kingdom. If we remain faithful, the power of this revelation will unite all generations.

Betrayal will either cause you to compromise the change or submit to those around you who say you cannot change. If you make the transition and come under criticism, you must remember not to become bitter, hurt, or wounded. It does not mean that those closest to you do not love you, they are just unwilling to change—that cannot deter you. Remember that only ten of the twelve tribes crossed over the Jordan. The two tribes that stayed behind were still a part of the family. The cost was too great for them at that time. When they were ready, they moved into the land and settled for whatever was left. When you move outside of God's timing, you will miss His perfect provision set aside for you.

It should be our goal to make every effort to live at peace with all men. But when it comes to change, we cannot afford to compromise. Change is a requirement for moving forward in God. The process of change is up to you. You can try to find the strength in yourself to work through the struggles of life by intellectual reasoning, leaving you empty, frustrated, and most likely causing you to repeat the lesson. Or, you can embrace the post and allow the Lord to change you. Stop looking at God's post as a stake of failure and realize that it is the foundation for accomplishing the success of God's purpose.

WHAT'S IN YOUR HEART?

As Paul returned to the post time and time again through the betrayals of his life, the Father's heart was refined within him. Through his journeys, he encountered a young man who became very valuable to him, and through this relationship we clearly see the purpose of the Father revealed. Paul carried the Father's heart toward Timothy. He shared with him the importance of hearing from the Father through the examples of his own struggles and his overcoming lifestyle.

> *This command I entrust to you, Timothy, my son, in accordance with the prophecies previously made concerning you, that by them you may fight the good fight, keeping faith and a good conscience, which some have rejected and suffered shipwreck in regard to their faith* (1 Timothy 1:18-19).

Timothy is entrusted with the experiences and teachings of Paul from the perspective of Paul's *heart* rather than his *knowledge*. He is encouraged to fight the good fight, keep the faith and a good conscience. Paul never let the betrayals of his life thwart the destiny God had given him. If he had, he never would have looked beyond his own generation. Today, we see generations being lost, but God is calling us to re-bridge the gap. Carry the Father's heart to sons and daughters, teaching them how to overcome the betrayals and rejections. Understand that God is refining you for your destiny so that He can establish His purposes in you.

107

Paul reminded Timothy of the prophecies that had been spoken over him. Words of direction had been given to Timothy that had not come to pass and Timothy was beginning to struggle. So often when a word is given to us and it does not fit at that moment, we throw it out as untrue. Instead, put it on a shelf and wait for God's timing to bring it to pass. You may find that the word comes alive at a later point in your life when you are once again at the stillness of the post, and that word empowers you to see beyond the moment. You see that God has already prepared you for what is ahead, and because of the prophecies, you are equipped to fight the good fight even in the face of betrayal.

I urge you to keep the faith. Hold on to what God has established in you, so that you will recognize the difference between God leading you to the post, and people who are trying to keep you bound in a place that is comfortable for them. No matter how unfamiliar or uncomfortable it may feel to your natural self, you must move forward with God's Spirit and be willing to change. God wants to take His Church beyond where it is today. Until you understand how to wage war and fight the good fight, you will remain tied to the post for training and growth. It is here that God establishes His paradigm in you and enlarges your vision to see from a greater perspective.

Chapter 8

PART OF LIFE

Betrayal is a fact of life—everyone has experienced it. Sometimes you will even walk through betrayal repeatedly from the same person. If we know who we are in Christ and we have spent time at the post being trained by the heart of God, why does betrayal continue to plague us?

Remember that betrayal began in the heavenlies when satan decided he would rule over God. This resulted in his ejection from Heaven when his attempt at anarchy failed. Cast down to earth, satan was powerless to betray the Father on his own again because he had made himself an enemy of God. Now, it was God's own image he would go after, because God had said, *"...let us make man in our image, according to our likeness; and let them rule..."* (Gen. 1:26). Through the enemy's deception and scheming, betrayal became the initial sin of man.

Although not directly spelled out in Scripture, there are fundamental conclusions we can draw from the life of Adam that expose the root of betrayal. It is obvious that Adam would have been the first whom satan would confront about the fruit, because we know that satan's primary goal is revenge toward the Father. As soon as satan could make creation turn against the Creator, he could go before the Throne with vile accusations of betrayal. Adam initially resisted because he was intimate with the Father. The Word clearly portrays Adam's relationship with God as one of close communion. His identity was his intimacy.

I believe that when Eve entered the picture, Adam's intimacy, and therefore his identity, shifted. He developed a greater intimacy with Eve than he had with the Father. The proof of this shift is evidenced when Eve fell for the enemy's deception and Adam failed to cover her sin. If Adam had stood firm in his identity with the Father, he could have approached God and taken responsibility for Eve's actions. He could have taken it upon himself and gone before the Father with humility and repentance. Instead, Adam cowardly ran away and hid himself, blamed Eve and ultimately blamed the Father for giving him the woman.

I believe that Adam could have stopped the betrayal at that point because of the way Scripture portrays Jesus. As the second Adam, Jesus accepted responsibility for the sin of man and took it upon Himself. Satan had successfully caused the first Adam to become a betrayer of God rather than a lover of God through shifting his intimacy from the Father to the created. In the wilderness experience outlined in Chapter 2, satan attempted the same manipulation with Jesus, but Jesus was rooted and grounded in His intimacy with the Father. He knew that the Father was the source of His identity. This allowed Him to carry out the perfect plans and purposes of God to the point of His own death. Jesus overcame betrayal so that we could have an example of trust.

Still, the reason betrayal is a part of life today is because the father of humanity made himself more important than God, and then tried to cast blame when the situation soured. He set in motion a generational curse that continues to infest the earth and its people. This curse is evident throughout Scripture beginning with Adam, exemplified in Ahab, revealed in Peter through his rebuke of Jesus, and apparent in countless other examples. Accounts of betrayal are like a scarlet thread woven throughout the ages and the world. The Word and world history are full of signs of the curse, but we need to look to further than ourselves. How many times have you made *your will* more important than *God's direction*, and ended up blaming God when things fell apart? It is all a result of the initial sin.

There are seasons when it seems that the act of betrayal is the goal of every person walking the planet—especially those around us. Offenses are rampant and there is an overall atmosphere of agitation. We betray someone and then end up being betrayed by someone else. Our perceptions are running on the super-sensitive setting. That is the key—many times betrayal is perceived and not based on fact. If we act on perceived betrayal and allow it to take root, it will produce bitterness within and become as damaging as intentional betrayal. We must understand that even in the face of betrayal, God will work through us for our good to develop His character.

TAKE UP THE MANDATE

The enemy will use various tactics in an effort to keep you from functioning in the purposes God has for you. Recognizing his attacks and examining your ways are strategic weapons of warfare that will help you to navigate the difficulties of life; still, they are not enough. When God gives you a mandate, it must penetrate your heart and become integrated into the core of your DNA, changing you from the inside out. Regardless of whether the mandate comes directly from the voice of God or God delivers it through someone you trust, a level of pursuit on your part is required to achieve the directives of the Father.

His mandate cannot be established only in your mind. Otherwise, the second the mandate is challenged, you will start questioning whether or not it is from God. You will stop trusting Him and start trusting in what other people say. Once that happens, the source of your identity shifts from the heart of the Father to the opinion of others. This becomes the breeding ground of betrayal. People will challenge God's direction because it goes against the carnal nature of humanity. Remember Peter rebuking Jesus because of His announcement that He would die? That announcement went against the selfishness of Peter's humanity.

Regardless of what the Lord sends us to do and no matter what comes into our life as a mandate from God, we must examine our lives to make sure that the character of Christ is being established in us. Then, as we begin to walk in that character, we will most likely encounter resistance—but do not be discouraged. After looking at the transformation of Paul in the previous chapter, we know that he of all people understood what it was like to walk triumphantly in the face of adversity. His advice to Timothy is just as applicable to us today. We must hold true to the faith, paying no attention to strange doctrines or useless conversations that do not further the Kingdom of God (see 1 Tim. 1:2-4). This is not always the most popular course of action.

As we obediently follow the instruction of God, we become a target for the darts of the enemy. We begin to feel the sharp "barbs" of pain and confusion as arrows poisoned with lies and accusations pierce our minds, telling us that we are not following the mandate correctly, or well enough, or even that we have missed it all together. If we allow the integrity of God in our life to be overcome by these arrows, then the fulfillment of our purpose will be jeopardized. We will experience problems in our lives and continue around the same mountain over and over again until we finally allow the truth of God to drench our heart like the Balm of Gilead, silencing the lies allowed in by the penetration of the poisonous darts.

Faith based on the Word of God will guide you through every situation that comes your way. By examining your heart and your ways daily, you will guard against the attacks of the enemy so that you will not be caught unaware and overtaken. This is what Paul meant when he told the Corinthians to, *"Test yourselves to see if you are in the faith; examine yourselves! Or do you not recognize this about yourselves, that Jesus Christ is in you—unless indeed you fail the test"* (2 Cor. 13:5). You must recognize Christ and His nature inside of you if you are going to be strong enough and wise enough to fulfill your destiny.

In order to fulfill the mandate God has given you, it must be so engrained within you that you walk in a level of love and faith that can only be attained through intimacy with the Father. You have to come to the point when life stops being solely about you. Mature love is characterized by giving. The love of Christ will propel you to see beyond yourself and realize that you are in a battle—a battle for your own eternal soul and the souls of others.

Fight the Good Fight

Timothy recognized that he was engaged in a spiritual war for the lives of men and women as he taught against vain reasoning and false doctrines. Paul admonished him to make sure that he gave instruction of *"love from a pure heart and a good conscience and a sincere faith..."* (1 Tim. 1:5). These are the three attributes of Christ that would empower Timothy to successfully influence and enable those whom God had placed in his charge:

- A pure heart. A heart unstained, unblemished, and innocent of personal will.

- A good conscience. Honestly doing all that God asks in order to establish His Kingdom.

- A sincere faith. Producing the character of God without having seen Him physically.

Instruction, advice, encouragement, and even correction that emanates from these virtues will carry the power of impact that produces positive change.

You are in a spiritual battle. Everyday the enemy will confront what you believe. There are people everywhere teaching, proclaiming, and discussing issues contrary to sound doctrine. If your identity is not grounded in Christ, you will be swayed by something that may sound good on the surface but is lacking the proper biblical foundation. A sound doctrine establishes the character of God; it is not a rule or regulation that only makes you look like you walk with God.

Build yourself up with teachings that establish Christ's character within you. As this happens, you destroy vain reasoning and speculations that come against the nature of God. When the nature and mind of Christ is set within you, you can begin to wield the weapons of warfare that are not made by man, but are, *"...divinely powerful for the destruction of fortresses... destroying speculations and every lofty thing raised up against the knowledge of God, and we are taking every thought captive to the obedience of Christ..."* (2 Cor. 10:3-5).

Before I met the Lord, I believed that my battle was with anyone who rose up against me. My strategy was to defend myself, disarming and overcoming any act of opposition. It was a violent way of life that produced very little substance or satisfaction. Even after I gave my life to Christ, there were many times that I had to fight off my natural survival instinct to retaliate against those who hurt my family or me. Today I understand that my enemy is not on the earth in human form. My enemy is satan and his cohorts. In the midst of the pain of betrayal and the struggles of everyday life, it is easy to lose sight of this truth.

Many times we are hurt or offended by people, intentionally or not, and we turn to our words or fists to defend ourselves. Even after we come to the realization that people are not the enemy, that we are in a spiritual war, it is difficult to shut down our natural reaction to return pain for pain. Anytime we choose to respond out of our flesh and enter into a fight with another person, we allow bitterness into our hearts. The war begins to rage between us—God's children—when He has called us to wage war against the enemy and walk at peace with each other. We must apply the Word of God to the situations that we encounter everyday so that He will become our source for overcoming each battle. This makes us victorious on two levels—first, we overcome our flesh; second, we overcome the enemy.

The Father went through betrayal, Christ went through betrayal, and we will go through betrayal. Whether betrayal changes us for better or for worse is our choice. We have been charged to finish the battle for our lives that began at the Cross. Specific, strategic weapons of warfare forged from a right relationship with Christ have been given to us. We must carry a victory mindset rather than one of negotiation. Walking with God is very simple, but it is not easy because it puts us in a constant state of opposition with our Adamic nature. The only way to be successful on this journey is to continually view life through the right perspective with the proper end in sight. Our objective is to establish God's character—His Kingdom—upon the face of the earth. In the midst of every battle, we must have knowledge and understanding of what God is working in our lives for the long term, rather than focus on a momentary struggle. We must have confidence that God will accomplish His plan and purpose in our lives.

BETRAYAL IS A TUTOR

Because of my past experiences, betrayal is not an enemy to me—I understand the place it has in my life. I trust that God is the source of my life and I have chosen to place full confidence in Him rather than in myself. When betrayal presents itself in my life, I view it as more of a tutor than a traitor or controlling force.

Much of what we walk through in life not only changes and refines us, but also provides opportunities to share with others. God will place people in our lives who will benefit from our experiences. They will learn from the struggles, the truths, the successes, and mistakes we have walked through, and they will go further in establishing the Kingdom of God. The same is true when we openly reveal the heartache of betrayal, the lessons learned, and the overcoming truth of Christ's love. God's plan and purpose for betrayal is for us to reveal to the world the differences between the natures of God and satan. God is concerned for our good; satan is only interested in his good and the destruction of God.

Through betrayal, we learn exactly what we are made of and how much of our life is based on our fallen nature versus the nature of Christ; we clearly see how much we are trusting in the Father and how many times we turn to our own abilities. This is one of the reasons that the Church has become a battlefield of betrayal—we have a wrong agenda. Even in the Church there is a *form* of godliness, but when it is put to the test, we fall back on our own nature instead of the nature of Christ.

We have become very adept at putting on a show or presenting a program that looks right and smells good, but it eventually cracks under pressure. When our good deeds do not stand the test of time, we end up feeling betrayed by the Church. In truth, deceitful spirits and doctrines of demons have led us from our faith in God to the place where our focus has become a religious program. The only way to walk in the provision and ways of God is to come to the place where our obedience to His purpose is being accomplished.

The enemy places betrayal in our lives in an attempt to divert our destiny. As Timothy took up his calling, betrayal began to affect him. He had been given a mandate to lay the proper foundation of offices in the church at Ephesus and he encountered a tremendous amount of struggle. The people rose up against him and began to challenge the direction from God. Soon, the work became a heavy yoke around his neck and the weight consumed him. Paul, Timothy's father in the faith, wrote to encourage him through the tears so that he would not lose sight of his purpose and quit (see 2 Tim. 1:3-6).

Anytime you begin to step out into what God has designed you to be and the work He has created for you to do, you will encounter struggles. Just as Paul encouraged Timothy, I urge you to remember that you are never beyond the Father's sight. He sees you day and night; He also sees the power and potential of your destiny. The struggles, the stretching, the process takes you to the next level. No fight you will ever be faced with is beyond God's nature in you. You cannot give in to the fears or the pain because diversion will keep you from God's desire for you, and it will also affect the lives of those whom you are called to serve.

"For God has not given us a spirit of timidity, but of power and love and discipline" (2 Tim. 1:7). No matter what situation you face, regardless of the severity of the betrayal, you are not alone. You can grasp hold of power, love, and discipline that the Father extends to you and stand your ground, face to face against the spirit of fear. Stop running from destiny because someone has hurt you and made you believe that you were incapable. When God fearfully and wonderfully crafted you, He did not include cowardliness so that you would run away from the struggle. You have been fortified with His Spirit and character so that you can walk through the battle.

Power and love beyond comprehension is your birthright. It is the very embrace of the Father, through the Son, to you. If you will release the pain and bitterness of betrayal, the power of the grace of God working in your life will change your character so that you will become a reflection of the Father. His love will encompass you, healing the open wounds of betrayal and allowing you to move past the pain.

Once you are touched by the Father's love, you begin to open yourself up to His discipline. This is an ability to be adjusted by the Spirit of God and by those who care for you. Without discipline and a willingness to become obedient to God, you will not complete the process of healing and restoration required to fully overcome betrayal. As our example, Christ learned obedience through suffering (see Heb. 5:8). Whenever you recognize adversity or hardship lurking around your house, look to see if it is actually discipline being used to establish a change in your character or your faith. Refusing to receive or walk out the discipline of God is the same as refusing to obey God; limited discipline means limited obedience.

LIMITED DISCIPLINE MEANS LIMITED OBEDIENCE

Limited obedience will cause you to speculate and reason in an effort to create a different option for yourself. You do not want to walk through the discipline that will refine you because of the accountability it will require. When you look at options to follow rather than obedience, people will lead you off course—you place yourself in a prime position for betrayal to enter your life. When it does, discipline is the only impediment that will stop betrayal. Discipline drives you back to the heart and presence of God the Father. Whenever you are willing to discipline yourself, you will not allow the purposes of God to be overcome by betrayal or rejection.

A few years ago, a precious couple in my life faced a test of discipline that caused them to choose between following the plans and purposes of God, or following a ministry platform and the acceptance of people. As the gap caused by differences in styles stretched to a canyon eroded by differences in paradigms, the defining line of God became clearly exposed. The couple could stay in the good graces of people, compromising what they believed to be God's mandate for their lives, or they could peaceably attempt to walk away in love. At great personal heartache, they chose the second option because ultimately, obedience to God is greater than any connection to others.

The months that followed were full of painful stabs and verbal accusations against their character. Thankfully, though, when you choose to walk in God's discipline, His love will shield you. Although you are facing betrayal, it does not penetrate you to the point of destruction. In fact, the accusations and betrayal brought against this couple only fueled their resolve to walk uprightly before God and become the "seed"—the generation to stop the cycle of betrayal between spiritual fathers and sons. Because they were willing to receive the discipline of God and to lay bare the human characteristics that had originally driven their choices, exchanging them for the correction of the Father; they are still moving forward today into greater depths of relationship and ministry.

Bear in mind that there are times when the leadership in your life makes a change that you may not always want. That does not mean that the person is wrong; it may just mean that you do not like the move, so you begin to fight it. Earlier in the chapter, the example of Timothy at Ephesus showed the people refusing to hear and rebelling against the instruction of the Word. As a result, Timothy began to back away from the grace and discipline of God, away from intimacy with the Father, because of the rejection of the people. That is when Paul reminded him that he did not have to cower to people who were not following the principles of God. As the leader, he needed to remain steadfast.

You cannot walk away because of struggles; in the same regard, the presence of a struggle does not necessarily mean you stay and push through. The difference in knowing when to remain and when to walk away is exposed as we examine ourselves according to His Word and His Spirit. Are we in the faith? Do we have a mandate, a plan and purpose from God? Are we open to the correction and discipline of God? As we examine ourselves, we will understand how satan uses betrayal as an avenue to lead us astray from the true character of Christ that is to be established.

Some people have the idea that if you are experiencing a struggle, you must not be following Christ or walking in a strong enough level of faith. However, if we use Paul as an example of a faithful son we see that although he had been beaten, shipwrecked, and imprisoned, he admonishes us to join with him in suffering for the Gospel (see 2 Tim. 1:8-9). I have seen many people walk away from struggles because they do not want to pay the price required for change. Anytime you walk away from the lesson God is trying to teach you, you will be brought back to the same place again and again—if you have a heart to serve God. You will return to the Post—the place of learning.

History teaches us that when the Spirit of God begins to work in a life, suffering will be experienced. No one particularly enjoys adversity, but be encouraged that you have not lost your mind, your faith, or your love for God. More importantly, God has not lost His love for you and He has not abandoned you. His power, love, and discipline enable you to overcome the struggle so that the struggle does not have to overcome you.

Paul encouraged Timothy not to be ashamed of trials or hardships because they are part of life. If you are going to walk with Jesus Christ, you will face betrayal and the suffering that accompanies it. Betrayal will come to deter you from your destiny. People and situations will be used to expose in whom you trust. It is your choice how the process of betrayal defines you.

The Word of God assures you that if you lose your life, you will find it; if you keep your life, you have already lost it (see Matt. 10:39). God's original plan was for man to be fruitful, multiply, subdue the earth, and to rule over it. In my book, *Spiritual Mentor*, you will find out that His plan has not changed. Everything we experience in life is driving us toward the fulfillment of this original mandate. God does not change His plan or purpose because we encounter a struggle. He sees us from eternity, not from the moment. God views every moment as history because He is the beginning and the end—He knows where we are headed. Because our loving Father has gone before us, we need to embrace the path ahead. The struggle makes us strong enough to face the future.

GOD'S WORK, NOT YOURS

Have you ever planned a special meeting or event? You confirm the dates, make the arrangements, prepare the food or travel plans, and fine-tune all the details—usually while sacrificing other tasks, personal energy, and sleep. Then when the big day or week finally arrives, few or no people show up and you are left with a dull ache of emptiness and failure. This is how it feels when you walk through a struggle. This is when you need to remember that the struggle was not some idea you had, to "Improve Your Life in 7 Steps." It was a tool that God used to deposit something in your life. Each step through the conflict was ordered by God as He led you through the refining process. The residual effect of betrayal is that God can trust you and you can trust God.

By walking through the struggle, you show that you are willing to be obedient and be purified. The Father proves that He will, "...*cause all things to work together for good to those who love God, to those who are called according to His purpose...*" (Rom. 8:28). God will turn the evil that the enemy has done to you into your good and the good of the Kingdom. He develops within you the very nature and character of His beloved Son, Jesus. Every time you face betrayal, it is an opportunity to experience a deeper level of trust in the Father, resulting in a greater manifestation of His character through you.

As you realize the purposes of God—the way He works through the struggles in your life—you will understand that the trials are rarely about you. In fact, it is pretty safe to say that they are never only about you. God moves in your life so that you will be able to share with others. Large, impenetrable obstacles in your life are broken down until they are merely a bump in the road for future generations. Every truth and provision God gives you is to be built upon and left as an inheritance for the next generations. This is the instruction that Paul gave Timothy: *"The things which you have heard from me in the presence of many witnesses, entrust these to faithful men, who will be able to teach others also"* (2 Tim. 2:2-5).

For too many years, we have been centered on a single generation. It is all about me, myself and I. With this viewpoint, we fail to see what long-term things God is doing in our lives, and we become entangled in our own personal struggles. It is time to realize that God is working in us in order to change the paradigms or mindsets of sons and daughters in the faith who will come after us. Future generations should not have to face the same struggles that we have faced. They will have struggles, but they do not have to repeat ours if we will fulfill our part in God's plan.

One step in fulfilling His purpose is to expose the process which betrayal takes you through in order to help others. Society pressures you to keep betrayal covered up because it would be shameful to let anyone know that you have major problems in your life, your business, or your family. You feel that you have to put on the "brave" smile while inside you are shriveling up and dying. This type of action is born out of the lies of self-pity in an attempt to cover up the fact that you are not perfect.

One of the most powerful ways to stop reliving the same adversity and put an end to the suffering is to stop taking everything so personally. Anytime we face difficult situations, our tendency is to zoom in on the trouble and forget about the world around us. Our attention feeds the situation and makes it larger than it really is. Instead, we need to keep in mind the bigger picture that our trials are meant to help strengthen others.

Betrayal pushes us outside our guidelines, outside the parameter of the rules of engagement. It is like walking down a narrow path, through a valley of land mines. The faster we move, the more mines we detonate. As a result, those who are following us become blasted with shrapnel and end up cut, bruised, and covered with wounds. If, on the other hand, we learn where to step in God's timing, accepting His instruction and discipline, we will make it through safely and those coming behind us will suffer fewer casualties. Anytime we walk through transition, we must ask God to help us view the situation through His eyes rather than trusting in our natural sight.

Betrayal is an internal modifier; it should instigate a heart change and a character change. Through the process, you will learn who you are and whether or not your trust is rooted and grounded in God. Betrayal itself is not consuming, rather it is the *effect* of betrayal that envelops all we are and hope to be. The purpose of going through betrayal is to take on the responsibility of changing our character to mirror the character of Christ so that we will examine ourselves with eyes that see clearly and a heart that seeks truth. We must come to the place where we can walk in the power of God, power which impacts our daily lives and helps us to overcome betrayal.

Holding on to a form of godliness rather than embracing His power will cause us to reshape the form so that it fits our own design rather than God's purpose. Once that happens, it can seem like we are right even when everything around us warns us that we are headed in the wrong direction. Truth becomes a blur because it does not fit into the reality we have created. We travel on down the yellow brick road of destruction, clutching feverishly to the false form while refusing God's power. Ultimately, we become the model of everything we hated and resisted in our lives.

After the scars of betrayal have been opened, we vow that we will never become a betrayer. But, without the power of God to burn out the infection and heal the open wounds, we become the embodiment of what we hate because it has been in us from the beginning. Paul describes our fate in Romans as, *"For what I am doing, I do not understand; for I am not practicing what I would like to do, but I am doing the very thing I hate"* (see Rom. 7:15-19).

Everyday life is all about waging war in the heavenlies, fighting the good fight, and being a finisher of the race. We are not walking in vain, experiencing the struggles of life without reason. Once we realize that the enemy wants to entrap us with his lies, we can expose him so that we are not identified by his lies. We will be empowered to stay the course, choosing to see the positive side of betrayal, which is the refining of Christ's character within us. With that, we will be able to walk through darkness to the light, pass through any struggle, and emerge victorious.

Chapter 9

SEEKING APPROVAL

Life is a journey based on an individual's search for identity and purpose. My life is a continuous search for God. Even though I have come to know Him, I constantly listen for His direction about where to go and what to say. I need to know His heart for every step I take on this path, every relationship I encounter, and every new dimension He calls me to.

We all hear God in various ways. Some people hear God through others, some through nature, and some through unfolding events. God uses a myriad of methods to communicate. The night I was saved, I heard God speak audibly as He called me by name and declared His love for me. The power and authority of His words shook the foundation of my life; but it was His penetrating love that shattered the coarseness and bitterness in my heart. He reached down into the abyss of emptiness within me to show me His sustaining love. He told me that He would put my feet on my destiny and show me wonderful things. Each time He speaks, there is a regeneration that comes to my spirit.

One of the most powerful times the Father spoke to me was in 1971. I was about ten days old in the faith, headed toward Flagstaff, Arizona. Minnie and I had stopped along the side of the road to eat some lunch. I sat alone on the tailgate mesmerized by this new reality and the wonderful experience of having met the Lord. The hell I had lived in and the struggle I had walked through seemed to be a lifetime ago. Christ had set me free and for the first time, there was peace and order in my life. It was almost too much for me to grasp.

As I sat there looking up into the sky, colors jumped out at me, the afternoon breeze gently brushed across my skin, and every fiber of my being surged with the strongest sense of being alive. I felt as if something tremendous was ahead of me. Instinctively, my spirit rested in the timelessness of the moment and I listened intently for the voice of God. I needed His direction; I had no idea what to do and I could only turn to Him.

Just then, the tailgate underneath me sagged from additional weight. I glanced over to see the Lord sitting right beside me. I can't describe how He looked, but I could sense that He was physically present. This may sound foolish to some who might ask why God would visit me this way—to this day, I do not understand it myself. All I do know is that as an unbeliever, I had been so vile and in such terrible shape that only an extremely dramatic visitation from God would secure my path in Him.

Sitting on the truck tailgate on the side of the road, the Father asked me if I loved Him. I sat motionless, searching for the right words until a simple response finally brushed past my lips, "Yes I do, Lord. I don't even know what that means, but I do." With a willing heart exposed, the Lord commissioned me, "I want you to tell My people who they are, where they are going and how to get there. Call My church to order." At the time, I had no idea what that meant—here today, I have walked with the Lord over 30 years and I still come back to what He said, daily at times. God is still unfolding the meaning of this powerful mandate.

All I heard that day was that God wanted me to deliver a specific message to people everywhere. Although I was completely dysfunctional in every way, He called me to speak His word to others. To say that I was a terrible communicator is being somewhat nice; in reality, I was introverted and extremely paranoid. I could not spell or even read the word "book," let alone deliver some meaningful sermon that would command the attention of masses of people. Although God had set me free, I was still haunted by my humanity and lack of skill to perform what He was asking. I found myself trying to tell Him, "No." I did not want to be a preacher; I did not want to tell anyone anything. I did not even like Christians. It seemed that they were always saying things that they did not mean and hurting each other. Quite frankly, I was tired of fighting and I had no idea how to tell people how to walk this journey; I could not even figure it out for myself.

Then, in a very simple, straight-forward manner, the Lord asked me if I loved Him. As I said, God speaks to each of us in many different ways. In my life, He has always been very straight to the point, very direct. So, when God asked me if I loved Him, the only answer I could give was the same one I had already given, "Yes." That settled the matter. If I truly loved Him, I needed to do what He had told me to do. My spirit, driven by love for this Savior, and my doubting human nature collided for what seemed to be an exhausting struggle, but must have been just a few seconds. I was overcome by how much the Father loved me and how much He loved His people. I finally said, "Yes, Lord, I'll do it—I'll tell Your people."

The truth I did not realize at the time was that many times when God speaks to us, He is speaking to our spirit self, not the outside shell that takes us through the journey of life. God speaks to our long-term destiny, not just the moment. Although there are times when He releases a word to soothe the circumstances that surround us or to calm the stormy seas, His mandate for our lives is about our created purpose. Whenever God is saying something to us it will reach into our lives and into the children of God—the sons and daughters—that we touch in our lifetime.

The mandate God had given me—to tell His people who they were, where they were going, how to get there, and to call them to order—began to permeate my life. That is when the testing began. Whenever God gives you a directive and you accept it, you will find yourself in a place where you begin trying to carry out whatever you see, feel, or sense God telling you.

As I began to pursue His mandate, I crashed full speed ahead into an obstacle called rejection. This is a manifestation of betrayal. When you believe that you have heard from God and people begin to reject your definition or your ability to hear Him, you become susceptible to the approval or disapproval of others—especially new believers. You find yourself in the position of trying to balance what you hear from the Lord and seeking the approval of people.

I have found that the more value I place in someone's opinion of me, the greater the voice of approval they have in my life. This can be very dangerous if it is not balanced with a right relationship with the Lord. Our first source of approval should always be the

Father. If God does not approve of us, the opinions of others are worthless. We must live our lives affirmed by God.

THE TIMING OF GOD

When we enter into a relationship with Christ, we are called to a supernatural walk that must be learned. We have to ascertain how to walk in the Spirit and not according to our own flesh. This is not very different from learning how to walk in the natural. There are times when we stumble and times when we are unable to get somewhere the way we want to get there. Along the way, there are plenty of spectators willing to give their opinion and critique. We must remember that the acceptance or rejection of others does not override the approval or affirmation of God. No matter what people say or do, it is imperative that we stay true to the calling of God throughout the entire process of learning to walk in the Spirit. God's perfect plan is often unveiled in a timing that may not fit our agenda. Acting prematurely can have grave consequences.

In the life of Samuel, God's timing and one man's belief could have changed the course of a nation if man's agenda had not prevailed. Samuel was a prophet of God who had judged Israel all of his life, traveling from city to city, functioning as the mouthpiece of God to the people. As he aged, it became clear that his sons were not following in his footsteps: *"His sons, however, did not walk in his ways, but turned aside after dishonest gain and took bribes and perverted justice"* (1 Sam. 8:3). Still, Samuel believed that his sons could be different.

Too many times when we hear the voice of the Lord, we do not wait on His timing for what He said to come about. If I were to write that I have always walked in complete maturity and function in the Lord from the day I started in the ministry to

131

this day, I would be lying. The fact is that I started in the ministry as a complete novice and at a very young age.

According to Scripture, and some people, I had no place out preaching the Word of God. I didn't come to Christ with a good "church upbringing" or even any strong sense of socially acceptable behavior. I lived by a code of self-preservation, where physical strength was more important than learning to read or write. Even so, God transformed me from an illiterate motorcycle gang enforcer to a man passionate for the heart of the Father. I knew then that I was called to fulfill destiny by sharing His Word and my testimony. In 1977, the miracle of God's transformation in my life was documented in the book, *Loco*.

When I came into ministry in the 1970s, at the end of the Jesus Movement, the trend was to give your testimony and share faith experiences with people. Because of my dramatic testimony, I was pushed into the spotlight too early. Consequently, whenever I held great meetings that encouraged the approval of people, I began to think too highly of myself. Within a short time, I had created a persona for myself that was larger than life. This attitude ultimately resulted in an act of betrayal that brought me back to the sincerity of the mandate that God had given me.

In a similar way, Samuel believed that his wayward sons could be turned back to God, but before that happened in God's timing, the people of Israel rejected the sons. They did not want to wait, and asked Samuel to appoint a king. Samuel felt betrayed. His perception was that he and his two sons were rejected. It is important for us to understand that God's timing and work in our lives is not always the way we would have it or the way others believe it should be.

Anytime we begin to seek the approval of people, we become blinded to the working of God and God's approval is nullified in our lives. We reject the work God is trying to do in and through us because it does not fit into other people's agendas. This is exactly what happened when the elders of Israel asked for a king to rule over them and judge them. They were rejecting God as King and Judge of the nation.

Samuel, as God's prophet, took offense from their request as he walked through the rejection of his sons. He had tried to convince the people that God would lead and guide his sons as judges if they would only have faith in the process. God would still speak to Israel through Samuel, and his two sons would grow into their responsibility. Still, the elders refused to wait, rejected God, and betrayed the provision God had assigned to their lives.

The leaders of Israel chose a king to rule over them rather than the design God had for them (see 1 Sam. 8:7-9). Israel rejected God's plan for them many times, in almost every stage that they had been through as a nation. The betrayal Samuel felt was real; in effect, the people were rejecting the mandate of God upon Samuel. They were rejecting the kingship of God upon the prophet and upon Israel as a nation. As a result, God made all kinds of requirements for Israel through the word of the prophet.

Under the reign of a king, Israel would have to make her sons build chariots. Daughters would become bakers and perfumers. The people would become servants of the king. He would take their crops, vineyards, and olive groves, along with a tenth of their seed and of everything they had. All that the people gave would be distributed to the king's officers. In other words, the king would first take care of the men who served him and the people would fend for themselves.

These were terms that Israel was willing to accept. Even today, I have found it to be true that everyone wants a king for the same reasons that Israel had centuries ago:

- Our fallen nature wants a natural king to rule us.

- Humanity looks to a natural king for position and identity.

- People seek a king's approval of their lives.

- People want a king to take responsibility for their actions.

- It is easier to blame a king when something goes wrong.

As we go through the struggles of life, it is very difficult to blame God for what comes to us through our own choices. In this example, our human nature is laid bare. We want a king to rule over us, no matter what the cost, so that there is always *someone else* to blame.

The cost for the people of Israel was very great. Instead of a king who fought for them, they served under a man who gave orders while they marched to the battle themselves. In the battle against the Amalekites, Saul was commanded to kill every living thing and destroy everything in the land. Still, he chose to disobey the Word of the Lord and brought back treasures, livestock, and the Amalekites' king. When Samuel rebuked him for this rebellion, Saul turned against the people and blamed them—another example of the cycle of betrayal. Those who betray eventually end up being betrayed by their own choices (see 1 Samuel 15).

APPROVAL THROUGH RELATIONSHIP

There are many times in your walk with God when you will hear the voice of the Lord as well as the persuasion of your flesh and the voices contradict each other. Ultimately, if you are seeking the approval of people or self versus God, it will lead to betrayal. There may be times in your life when you put such a high value on other people's opinions and approval that their word of rejection will cause you to reject God.

The tragedy of betrayal is that if you cannot see beyond the moment of betrayal, you will become a betrayer. When you are validated and approved by God, you place the opinion of people in the *proper perspective*. As a believer, I think you should always be open to hear others. The Bible makes it clear that there is wisdom in a multitude of counsel. It is helpful to have people in your life who will share the truth with you. Still, you are the one who is accountable to God to seek His approval above all things. If this does not happen, people will become your god or a king in your life. It is a natural tendency to seek the approval of friends, family or coworkers, rather than the approval of God because somehow it seems easier to measure with our human emotions. This hazardous pursuit, though, will manifest betrayal in your life almost every time.

Understand that there is a major difference between hearing someone's counsel and seeking their approval. Sometimes I am concerned about telling people so firmly that the bottom line is accountability to God, because it can be taken to an extreme. Approval must come from God because He is the one who judges each of us. Confirmation and affirmation can come from others, but not judgment. The approval of God is based on His love, which acts as a penetrating band flowing around the heart of believers. The love of God so encompasses your mistakes that He will work them out for your good (see Rom. 8:28). Even if you miss God's prompting, the Spirit of God loves you enough that He will put His arms around you and direct you back to the right path.

Anytime we seek the approval of men in order to find the right direction for our lives, we will end up making mistakes. This does not mean that we should not place value on the opinion of men or women who love us. God creates divine connections in our lives with those who will walk with us, speak to our destiny, and carry the Father's heart toward us. Only someone who loves you can truly watch for your life or care for you. This requires establishing a relationship.

One of the reasons betrayal is so intimately devastating is that, in order to have approval, you must be vulnerable. Therein lies the tragedy—when trust is betrayed, the razor rips directly through exposed flesh because your defenses have been removed. To know the approval of God, you must have relationship with God. Relationship is also required to gain the approval of people. Without relationship, you place no value on whether someone approves or disapproves of your decisions.

When you have a relationship with the Lord, passion will compel you to study His Word and reach out to Him to find out what it is He is asking you to do to fulfill the mandate He has spoken over your life. Relationship is the fundamental building block of this quest. You must harbor God's love in your heart and reciprocate His love. Communication and interaction enjoyed in His presence will strengthen your sensitivity to His presence and His direction for your life. If you do not have a sufficient relationship with God, you will value the opinion of others more than the approval of God.

Once you begin to look to others for validation, you have stepped onto a thin sheet of ice. Life is not easy and betrayal is not a slap on the wrist. If anyone tells you that overcoming betrayal is easy, they are lying to you. If you think that it will not come into your life, you are lying to yourself. Your job will betray you, the world will betray you, even your family will betray you—not once, but many times during your life. The only protection you have to help you walk victoriously through betrayal is to have an intimate relationship with God.

THE POWER OF APPROVAL

Peter is one of the greatest examples in Scripture of someone with an intimate relationship with the Father. After all he walked through with Jesus, even after he had betrayed the Lord, he boldly walked as one having the approval of God. He had a relationship that withstood the betrayals and he fully understood his destiny. Remember that Peter had received a powerful revelation of who Jesus was, and then rebuked Him for prophesying death on the Cross. He betrayed the Lord again by denying Him in the courtyard after the soldiers had taken Him away. Still, after the death and resurrection of Jesus, Peter became zealous in fulfilling the great commission to preach the Gospel. He and John were thrown in jail for preaching and were brought before the high court to be questioned (Acts 4:1-3).

Peter, being full of the Holy Spirit, boldly proclaimed the salvation of the Lord before the elders of the high council and they become furious. He did not dilute the power or significance of the miracles that had been done in the name of Jesus and he did not let the rejection of these spiritual leaders divert him from his purpose. This attitude greatly disturbed the high priests. They knew that thousands of people were accepting Jesus of Nazareth, the same man they had rejected, persecuted, and killed. Now, two of Jesus' disciples stood before them to repay the act of betrayal that they had inflicted upon the approved Son of God.

The response of fallen man would be to repay evil for evil, mocking the high priests by giving an account of the revolution sparked by Jesus' death. Instead, Peter and John expose the heart of the Father by telling the high priests that they were the ones the Messiah had come for originally. Even though they had cried out for Jesus' death, they could now cry out to Him as Lord and be saved. Imagine the boldness of this moment in history. Peter and John faced the very men who had led the revolt against their Master, and yet they shared the Master's love for them.

Sometimes betrayal will come because of the acceptance or rejection of a multitude of people. This is why it is imperative to know that you have the approval of God and know Who He is that has sent you. This is your defense against betrayal. When the calling and purposes of God have convicted your heart, you must follow His direction. You need to find the will of God and pursue it no matter what it is and no matter how many people reject it, because at the end of the day, you are accountable to God alone.

This conviction of heart was the same defense Peter and John used when they said, *"... Whether it is right in the sight of God to give heed to you rather than to God, you be the judge, for we cannot stop speaking about what we have seen and heard..."* (Acts 4:19-20). The only answer you can give to people who reject you when you are carrying out the plan for your life is, "Should I do what you tell me or what God tells me?" The answer is clear. To live a life of conviction, we must follow what we have seen and heard from the Father; this assignment can only be attained through relationship. The greater your relationship, the more you are empowered to fulfill your purpose.

A CONVICTED HEART

Once God revealed a purpose to me through His mandate to tell His people who they are, where they are going, how to get there, and to come to order, conviction was birthed in my spirit. The longer I have walked with Him, the more I am convinced that not only what I have heard and seen is real, but that the fruit is real as well. The fruit in my life is the reality of all that God has shown me and spoken to me through the years. First, I had to be convinced in my heart that my God was able. Within six months, I learned to read and write well enough to pass the High School Equivalency Exam so that I could go on to college.

The Spirit of God empowered me to successfully accomplish what I could never attain on my own, and He did it using His method and in His timing. The Lord told me that if I would pray and read His Word six hours a day, He would bring me to a place where I could speak revelation knowledge to His people. This would have been a simple task if I could have read anything. For hours I would put my finger on the Bible and pray in the Spirit over letters that were nothing more than black lines filling ivory paper. As I prayed, God would supernaturally reveal to me the meaning of the words. My wife, Minnie, helped me learn the alphabet and phonics so that I could pronounce and enunciate words properly. Ultimately, it was the power of God that transformed my willing heart into a life that could be used for His glory.

God's work in my life of imparting wisdom and enabling skills affirmed the reality of what He was speaking over my life. His approval burned a relentless passion within me. The rejection of people is inconsequential compared to the greatness of pleasing my Father. People have rejected me many times. I have heard that I am not a preacher and that I am too harsh, but the conviction of God in my life causes me to drive forward and do what He has called me to do.

Whenever you decide that you are willing to pay any cost to do what God has told you to do, you will encounter a true test of character as you begin to pursue God. Obedience to God does not deter rejection or betrayal. In fact, many times when you stand firm in your convictions people will reject you all the more. Those who live by conviction of heart will generally incur betrayal, but it is that conviction that strengthens you through the struggle. That which convicts you will save your life from betrayal because it causes you to act out of a trust in the Father that goes beyond all you understand. You are seeking His approval in your life, and none other.

THE THINGS THAT CONVICT YOU SAVE YOU FROM BETRAYAL

The mandate Jesus gave me on the tailgate of my truck has always been before me. Since then I have faced betrayal a number of times. Sometimes, I overcame it successfully by trusting the Father and continuing to move forward. Other times, I was overcome by deep, penetrating wounds of betrayal that left me stripped and barren. Several times, the betrayal came as a direct result of acting on my convictions. My convictions make me vulnerable to people who have no conviction—people who test the wind to see were they stand—because they will change their stance in the midst of walking beside you.

We all are a work in progress—God will never stop working in our lives and changing us. What we need is the approval of the One we value the most. His name is Jesus the Christ, the Lover of our soul.

Chapter 10

ANTIDOTE FOR BETRAYAL

Throughout this book I have shared personal accounts of betrayal, both perceived and real. Each act of betrayal was built upon the last, creating a wall of defense that surrounded my heart. I had to seclude myself in order to avoid repeating the process of betrayal toward others, and I instinctively hid away any vulnerability that would allow someone to hurt or wound me again. In this fractured capacity, I found a way to continue to function in the faith without getting close enough to believers to risk being wounded by rejection. People would come into my life and even share parts of it, but they would never actually touch my life. That way, no one would be hurt.

My past experiences dictated my responses to present and future situations. I refused to put my family, my wife and daughter, in a place where they could be wounded again, and I was determined to do whatever it took to protect them and myself. That is when the wall I had built to keep people out became a prison cell that enclosed me. In that guarded and secure place, God spoke to my heart with healing and restoration to put me back on the course of destiny. He asked a simple question, "Are you willing to take the wall down and become vulnerable?" With my back against the wall, it seemed that what He was asking of me would be too great. I said, "No." Still, the Father continued to embrace me with His love.

Within time, I began to see that the barricade I had built to keep others out had also blocked His touch from my heart. The book, *Spiritual Mentor*, came out of my vulnerability toward God once the wall was destroyed. Sometimes we are so focused on what is happening to us that we never consider how our lives affect others. Applying the antidote for betrayal will stop its venom from contaminating the people around us.

Antidote is defined as a "substance that counteracts the effects of a poison or a disease." Betrayal cannot be pushed away or swept under the rug, it requires an antidote. We must apply something that will stop us from reproducing the poison that enters our lives through betrayal.

THE POWER TO SERVE

Whenever you have a wall built up in your life, to any degree, you are choking out a release of the fullness of God over your life. Once the wall is removed and you begin to yield to the Father—not only to His correction but also to His embrace—you will experience a greater presence of God. This will ignite a stronger desire to help and serve other people. You begin to look for ways to walk with people rather than stay in a place of rejection where they are cut off. Too many times, that search turns into a quest for position. So, a counteraction to betrayal—a key to keep you from reproducing betrayal—is to stop looking for position and start looking for function.

Betrayal Antidote Ingredient: Servanthood

Matthew gives us a profound example of two men seeking position without having the necessary character. James and John, the sons of Zebedee, sent their mother to Jesus to petition Him on their behalf. As a distant relative, she had an entrance with Jesus, so she asked Him if her two sons could sit on either side of Him in Heaven (see Matt. 20:21-22). You may read this passage and wonder how someone could be so pretentious, but before labeling her as bold and assuming, consider what drove her to petition Jesus. Our human nature is always looking for position, title, or notoriety—a place of authority. The higher the stature you have, the more people accept you and want to hear what you have to say. It is an innate desire in us to have a position of acceptance. This mother simply wanted the best for her sons.

Jesus said, *"You do not know what you are asking for. Are you able to drink of the cup that I am about to drink?"* (Matt. 20:22). Although He was responding to the mother's question, he was speaking to James and John. They had no idea how much it would cost to be seated on either side of the Messiah. In their ignorance they replied that they were able to drink from the same cup. Jesus was referring to the cup of guile, the cup of rejection, which was given to Him while hanging on the Cross.

James and John were told that they would certainly drink of the same cup, but only the Father could determine who would sit beside Christ. Jesus did not have the ability to fulfill the request because only the Father knew the thoughts and intents of their heart. Still, the other disciples became indignant with the brothers for their request and for using their mother in an

143

attempt to gain position (see Matt. 20:24). Each of them wanted the distinction of being the closest one to the Lord and compared themselves with each other to ascertain who was more eligible for this position.

We still go through this ritual today. We look at other people and compare ourselves to them in an effort to make ourselves look or feel better. We are always going around trying to find the best seat and, inevitably, we end up standing in the back. Christ tells us in Scripture that it is better to take a lesser seat and be called up to the front rather than be removed from the seat of pre-eminence (Matt. 23:3-12).

This passage in Scripture exemplifies how much God desires us to deal with our fallen nature and examine the motivations behind what we do. He uses this situation as an opportunity to teach the twelve disciples an important truth about how to overcome betrayal. Jesus talks about how the rulers of the Gentiles lorded over them, always looking for a position of rule so that they could exercise authority over the people. Although this is a common state for people, it should not be that way among believers. Instead, we should take on the understanding that greatness is born out of being a servant, and becoming first comes from being a slave. Using Himself as an example, Jesus told the disciples, *"...the Son of man did not come to be served, but to serve, and to give His life as a ransom for many"* (Matt. 20:26-28).

In order to overcome betrayal without reproducing it, you must have the heart of a servant. If your desire is to be a man or woman of notability and authority, you must first be a servant dedicated to caring for others rather than establishing position. Jesus is the greatest example of this paradigm in that, *"although He existed in the form of God,* [He] *did not regard equality with God as a thing to be grasped..."* (Phil. 2:6). God wants you to fully understand His example so that you will become an example yourself. Jesus emptied Himself and became a bond-slave to the will of the Father. This is how He dealt with betrayal.

The motives of your heart, not the outworking of your actions, determine your true place of authority in life. In Chapter 2, "Process of Betrayal," the account of Cain and Abel was outlined in detail. Their act of sacrifice, though similar on the outside, was clearly fueled by entirely different motives. Both Cain and Abel brought an offering to God. Cain's offering, given to affirm a position of self, was rejected by God. Abel's offering was given as a sacrifice, asking for relationship rather than position, and God accepted it. Seeking relationship with the Father will establish the heart of a servant within you. Stop looking for notability and acceptance from other people and find a way to carry the Father's heart to others. If you take on the heart of a servant, just as Jesus did, you carry the antidote for betrayal.

The antidote for betrayal is desperately needed everywhere. The world, the marketplace, even the Church is inundated with this plague. It is the nature of satan to betray and anytime he infiltrates people's hearts, he will institute a craving for authority and position so that they will lift themselves above others. Self-exaltation is a primary attribute that we must recognize and deal with so that we do not reproduce it. The heart of a servant counteracts this faction of our fallen nature, and seeks the will of the Master.

BE A WISE SERVANT

It is hard to walk in a state of humility, having a servant's heart, in a world where people continually strive to exalt themselves, vying for position. I am not equating humility with being a doormat, allowing people to walk all over you. The reality is that if you do not want betrayal in your life, you have to watch out for people who will attempt to use you in order to distinguish themselves. When their agenda crosses with yours, betrayal will manifest. The antidote is to keep a servant's heart that does not try to prove your position or impose your will. If you have been betrayed in a situation, applying the antidote of servanthood will bear witness of the good that is in you—without having to say a word. *"...Every good tree bears good fruit, but the bad tree bears bad fruit"* (Matt. 7:15-17). Rest assured that your works will prove what is in your heart. Anytime you come across a true servant, you will find a heart that is passionately seeking God.

Betrayal Antidote Ingredient: Humility

One of the major problems in society today is man's desire to propagate his own agenda in order to achieve position. It does not matter what title you have—ministry or secular—God will always reject the sacrifice of the proud that is given to obtain prominence. Many believers busy themselves with the things of God in an effort to catch the accolades of men, but Scripture clearly states, *"Not everyone who says to me, 'Lord, Lord,' will enter into the Kingdom of heaven; but he who does the will of My Father in heaven will enter"* (Matt. 7:21). There are many acts done in the name of the Lord that have absolutely nothing to do with the Kingdom. The will of the Father is for each of us to become a servant, not a master or ruler. True leaders administer out of a heart to serve; it is not about them, it is about the people.

Throughout our lives, we are taught lessons about great men and women who ruled countries and people groups, built businesses and established nations. Still, the simple truth is that the greatest in the Kingdom of God is not a person of nobility who exalts himself; it is the person who serves. This should be a lesson that helps you identify the proper timing of God so that you will be able to discern whether someone is in your life to serve you or if they desire to be served. Remember, the teacher never comes until the student is ready because it is not about the teacher.

The public educational system in our country is full of teachers with agendas that have nothing to do with preparing students to function in today's society. They carry personal agendas, trying to implement their ideals into young, impressionable minds. A true teacher is focused on preparing the student and serving the student's destiny rather than fulfilling personal motives.

Personal agendas are circulated in the church world as well. How many people have you encountered who have the "word of the Lord" for you? It seems that every time I turn around there is someone who has a word from God, just for me. I am not saying that you should shut yourself off from people, but you must use wisdom in perceiving whether their motive is to serve your destiny or to create a position of self-importance. Some personal prophecies are more about personal agendas than what God is actually saying in order to bring you to the place He wants you to be. You need to be wary of prophecies that proclaim position—this is an ingredient of betrayal. It may not sound or look like that in the beginning, but a little way down the road, betrayal will reveal itself.

If you are the one with a word of prophecy, make sure that there is no element of desire to establish your own position in someone else's life. In Matthew, the people Jesus refers to were trying to enter the Kingdom of Heaven, saying, *"...in Your name we cast out devils..."* (Matt. 7:21) and Jesus responded with, *"...I never knew you; depart from Me, you who practice lawlessness..."* (Matt. 7:23). Anytime your actions are driven by a desire to be noticed, you need to take a step back and reevaluate your heart before God. Acting out of self in order to establish position creates a fertile seedbed for betrayal.

Again, these are symptomatic situations warning you that betrayal could be coming—they do not mean that betrayal will come. Be careful not to judge everything that is said to you as evil and everyone who comes to you as a betrayer. Sometimes, a person may simply be giving you a word of encouragement. Ground yourself in the Word of God to test what is spoken to you and let go of the rest. If you have a good idea or concept, take it to the Father first. Test it to see if it serves destiny or self. Any act that serves to position or exalt man is the beginning work of betrayal. Any act promoting destiny is born out of a wise servant.

To Love or Not To Love

Life is like a chess match; we are pawns choosing to be representatives of either the Kingdom of Light or the kingdom of darkness—the Kingdom of Love or the kingdom of hate.

In the New Testament, Paul writes instructions about gifts of teaching and prophecy, miracles, and the five ascension gifts. He admonishes us to earnestly desire greater gifts, but he emphasizes a more excellent way—love (see 1 Cor. 12–13). Love is the greatest antidote that we have in relationship to the Kingdom of Light. We can understand prophecies, mysteries and gifts of knowledge and have faith that moves mountains, but in the end we are nothing if we do not have love. The antidote that destroys the poison of betrayal is love.

Over the years, many ministers have expended great amounts of energy teaching the "Love Chapter" (1 Cor. 13). Take a moment to study the following passage with the understanding of love's powerful ability to destroy the ravaging effects of betrayal:

> Love is patient, love is kind and is not jealous; love does not brag, and
> is not arrogant, does not act unbecomingly; it does not seek its own, is
> not provoked, does not take into account a wrong suffered, does not

rejoice in unrighteousness, but rejoices with the truth; bears all things, believes all things, hopes all things, endures all things. Love never fails... (1 Corinthians 13:4-8).

How do we apply this attitude of love in a practical way? How do we transform this from a statement on the page to strength in our character?

I struggled with the word "love" for years. Though it is extremely simple, it is not easily invoked. Love requires us to step outside of ourselves, to step outside of our own humanity. In order to fully experience love, we must walk in the Spirit and see things in a different way. We have all experienced betrayal, whether by a job or business, partners or employers, church people or ministries, families or friends. Rejection or betrayal is a part of life, everyday. If it is not dealt with properly, bitterness takes root in our spirit. In order to overcome the force of betrayal, the antidotes of serving and love must be practically applied to our lives. This requires accepting a new level of maturity.

Betrayal Antidote Ingredient: Love

The power of love outlined in the passage in First Corinthians chapter 13 will transform your life only when you realize that you are required to act upon it in the midst of every circumstance in your life. *"When I was a child, I used to speak as a child, think as a child, reasoned as a child: when I became a man, I did away with childish things"* (1 Cor. 13:11). One of the struggles the Church has is coming out of childhood into a place of maturity in living and walking by the Spirit. It is in our fallen nature to demand that life be on our terms; we want our way. God says that if we are going to come into the place He has designed, we must put away childish things. Love activates trust. When you walk in the maturity of love, you will choose to trust the Father rather than relying on someone else to identify you and create a place for you. When you trust the Father, you walk in the fruit of the Spirit, fully exhibiting the activating force of love in your life.

Galatians 5 outlines the significance of walking out your life according to the Spirit of God. Whenever you follow after your flesh, it is easy to become boastful and look for a place to position yourself. This opens the door to betrayal. One of the characteristics betrayal presents is *envy*; either envy is manifested toward you or you are the one manifesting it. Envy is a destructive force that can only be abolished by love and living by the Spirit of God: *"If we live by the Spirit, let us also walk by the Spirit. Let us not become boastful, challenging one another, envying one another"* (Gal. 5:25-26). This is not always easy to carry out because of the extreme opposition between the Spirit and our flesh.

We are in a battle where spirit contends against flesh and flesh wars against spirit. They do not want any part of each other. The reality of the presence of God challenges the rules and regulations of man and the carnal desires of our flesh. Unattended betrayal in your life is evidenced by deeds of the flesh that are rooted in bitterness, *"...immorality, impurity, sensuality, idolatry, sorcery, enmities, strife, jealousy, outbursts of anger, disputes, dissensions, factions, envying, drunkenness, carousing and things like these..."* (Gal. 5:19-21).

These issues deal with your personal character and are a result of betrayal in your life; either you are betraying others and you cannot see beyond their struggle, or someone is betraying you and he or she does not see beyond your struggle. The resulting action is that one person, either you or the person betraying you, is positioning themselves as the one entitled to correct the situation. That person is attempting to force a personal agenda on another. This is what betrayal looks like; it deals only with the moment. Love looks beyond the moment.

Betrayal deals only with the moment; love looks beyond the moment.

My struggle with love came from defensively trying to protect myself while walking in love at the same time. This is impossible, because love in its very conception is vulnerable. One of the keys that unlocked my freedom from betrayal was the ability to look beyond the incident of the offense. I began to look at people, not with my human eyes, but through the eyes of God. This ability can only come out of intimacy with the Father.

Intimacy is not just about feeling desired or wanted by God because He has enclosed us in His embrace. It is more than feeling appreciated or good about ourselves and passing that feeling of acceptance on to others. True intimacy is about being infused with His passion. When you are driven by the passion of the Father, you are empowered to look beyond the moment of pain and treachery and see with compassion the purposes of God. The antidote of love totally eradicates the poison of betrayal because it goes deeper than the suffering.

The only way to walk through life without becoming gripped with bitterness through betrayal is to apply love to the offense. Look beyond the act and see the other side. Sometimes it is beyond your capacity to do this in your own strength. You need the power of God to bring complete healing and restore you to a relationship with your First Love. Keep in mind that this is a process. It is not about your works or even your will to move beyond the pain; healing comes out of the heart of the Father.

When God told me to tear down the wall and return to Him, I still struggled with releasing the agonizing affliction. I could not simply let it go. Then, my eyes were opened to the reality that I had become the personification of what I detested—I saw myself as the betrayer.

One day my wife came home from church very distressed. When I asked her how church had been, she said, "You don't want to know." When I looked into her eyes, I became almost angry as I said, "I do want to know." Minnie looked back at me and with tears silently dripping down her face, she replied, "I'm dying. If you don't teach me, I will die." Her response was not because of the betrayal that had come to our lives and ended with us living in a garage; it was because of my betrayal toward her. I had stopped covering my wife and daughter with love and had turned all of my attention inward. The two most important people in my life took a secondary place behind the pain and struggle caused by betrayal.

When Minnie said that she was weak and losing faith because my betrayal was tearing at her spirit, my heart was struck by lightening. The power of love to destroy the wickedness of betrayal and rejection and all of its effects surged through me. I looked at her and said, "I will. I will teach you." Even when I said it, I did not want to do it. I still wanted to cling to my own struggle. Yet, I watched the Father take my decision and begin to turn my life around.

It only takes a choice—a decision to say, "No. I will not let bitterness or betrayal control me. I am going to give of my life and of what God has given me." Once I made the commitment in my mind and resolved in my spirit to follow through, the love the Lord had put into my heart for my wife and daughter was rekindled inside of me and we began to overcome the effects of the terrible event in our lives. It is not easy. To love at your expense is to love God's way. It requires you to reach beyond yourself, to see beyond the moment and serve others.

I had to change the course of events I went through because the betrayal in my life brought me to where I am today. Through the trials, God has equipped me to carry the love of the Father in a way so far beyond my comprehension that it is even difficult for me to articulate it enough to share with people. Still, I know that I carry His love and His heart in a manner which I would never have been able to if it had not been for the betrayal that was overcome by love in my life.

Antidote Ingredients:

- Servanthood

- Humility

- Love

- Perspective

This betrayal antidote is the most potent and effective balm that exists. When you cry out to God and see that something greater than the pain is being accomplished in your life, you will walk through situations saying, "It is not I, but Christ; it is not about me, but His people." Then, you will join with countless others who are overcoming the works of betrayal, and becoming stronger because of it, everyday.

Chapter 11

TRUTH OR PERCEPTION

Everywhere I go, people ask me how to hear the voice of God. How do you know what God is really saying and what His purpose is for your life? I have spent years listening for the voice of God in every area of my life. My greatest assets in this endeavor are the ability to *be still*, to *cease doing* things on my own, and to actually *hear* what the Lord is saying. Also, I realize that I must walk according to truth and not out of my perception of the truth. In order to do that, my ear must be tuned to the Spirit of God.

Too many times, we miss what God is actually saying in a situation because we stop short of listening and accept what is spoken only on the surface. Everything Jesus learned to do, He learned from His Father. His first priority was communication with the Father and spending more time with Him than anyone else. This is a foundational key we must take hold of and appropriate in our lives. We must be able to come to the place where we can *"...be still and know..."* that He is God (see Ps. 46:10 KJV). Communication is being able to hear God, not only talk to Him. This is the most important factor in discerning the truth in any situation.

Often, betrayal is birthed out of a situation that begins with perceived betrayal simply because someone believes that they have a better idea—it is not the intent of their heart to betray. There are two dynamics that happen—that of the betrayed and the betrayer. Whenever people try to assert their opinion, you may perceive their actions as betrayal based on your past experiences. In the same sense, a betrayer may assert his or her opinion as a suggestion of what should happen based on conversation or observations. In either case, without the illumination of truth by the Spirit of God, one party or both will cause the perception of betrayal to become a full act of betrayal.

This is exactly what happened with Judas and his betrayal of Christ. During the Last Supper, Jesus disclosed the fact that He would be betrayed by one of the disciples. They looked at each other, questioning who could do such a thing. Then Jesus said, *"...that is the one for whom I shall dip the morsel and give it to him..."* and He gave the bread to Judas with the instruction, *"...what you do, do quickly."* Those at the table completely missed what Jesus was saying to Judas and presumed that He was just referring to money matters. When Judas left, they thought nothing of it (see John 13:21-30).

In reality, an element had passed between Judas and Jesus that is vitally important for us to understand in relationship to betrayal. There is the fact of betrayal and there is the perception of betrayal. Judas Iscariot was a zealot; his heart was not set on betraying Christ. Judas belonged to a sect of people who were committed to the overthrow of the Roman Empire and the establishment of the Jewish nation as the ruling people. When he listened to the statements Jesus made with his human heart and the perception of his carnal man, it fueled his passion. Statements like, *"The kingdom of God is at hand,"* combined with the principles Jesus taught, served the agenda Judas lived for because he heard Jesus speaking through his own personal perception. Judas wanted Jesus to set up an earthly Kingdom. When we understand the elements of Judas' nature, we can imagine that he looked at Christ and interpreted His words based on his personal political agenda. So, when Jesus began talking about His death, it did not fit into the picture Judas had for the future.

THE **FACT** OF BETRAYAL AND THE **PERCEPTION** OF BETRAYAL

Sometimes when God begins to direct our lives and work through us, we are faced with the challenge of laying down our own ideas in order to take up His mandate. This can prove to be very difficult because there are times when we feel that we know just how things should be done. We must come to the place where we hear what God is saying through His Spirit rather than our spirit of flesh. Many times betrayal enters into our lives because of what we think is going on based on our perceptions rather than the truth of what is actually happening.

Discerning the motives behind the actions of others can be very complicated. If we look at others with open honesty, first we need to deal with the truth of our own hearts. In the example of Judas, the Word does not indicate that he sat down with the Lord in a heart-to-heart conversation and said, "What you need to do is set up Your kingdom and yet You keep telling me that You are going to die. That will not work. We are here to rule and reign and set up a Jewish kingdom; you are working toward something different." Still, this was the perception Judas carried and, consequently, all of his actions were driven by his conviction to see that kingdom established.

Judas' mindset was such that he believed the Pharisees would seize Jesus and then Jesus would be forced to set up His kingdom. I believe that in his heart Judas thought that Jesus was the Christ, the Son of God, and that He should reign. So, he was going to help spur Him into action. I don't think it was an intentional act of betrayal, based on later Scripture that tells us that Judas became sorrowful unto death when he realized what he had done. You can see here how perception plays such a critical role in our lives. Judas' perception set destiny into motion and culminated in Jesus bearing the brunt of betrayal that had begun in the heavenlies.

When Judas walked out the door, Jesus knew that betrayal had been set in action; that is what He meant when He said, *"...now is the Son of man glorified and God is glorified in Him..."* (John 13:31-32). He understood that perception would become factual betrayal because of Judas' desire to assert his own will. Still, He did not take the anguish into His heart. Jesus did not get angry, frustrated, or condemn Judas to hell. He knew that betrayal would come and once it did, He remained steadfast because He trusted the Father and was able to see through the Father's eyes. That is how He could say that the Son of man and the Father would be glorified. Christ knew that He must walk the course in order to establish a timeless Kingdom that would change the paradigm.

ESSENTIAL TRUTHS OF BETRAYAL

Today, as men and women of God, we have been given the mandate to occupy the earth with the presence of the living God. When you look at betrayal and ask, "What have I done wrong, why am I going through this?" you are allowing a perception to control your destiny. You let the experience of betrayal define your limitations in your exploits for God. This perception becomes so real that you cannot see the heart of the Father anymore. You become blinded to your destiny and purpose. The plan of God for your life is undone because you allow the view of betrayal to become so prominent that you cannot see clearly.

You must understand that betrayal will come to everyone. People base so much of their lives on the past, but where you have been is only a springboard for where you are going. Your history does not define your destiny. Therefore, past experiences have no power to control where you are currently or where you will go from here. Adopting this mindset will enable you to grow through the process of betrayal so that you become stronger in your purpose and more sensitive to the heart of the Father. There are four essential truths you learn through betrayal:

- Jesus understands what we as humans do not—the struggle is what makes the presence of God valuable.

- The word *through* is the key to all that we experience.

- The answer to overcoming betrayal is to love at our own expense.

- To effectively overcome betrayal, we must see through God's eyes.

1. **Jesus understands what we as humans do not—*the struggle is what makes the presence of God valuable.***

   Jesus told the disciples that they would face struggles after He left. These struggles would be the tools that reveal the value of God's presence. Because of our fallen state, people face struggles of various degrees and through different circumstances everyday. We have a tendency to become bitter and lock ourselves away whenever we are stung by the poisonous darts of betrayal. However, if we drive *through* the struggle and begin to see the problem—that we are walking through either the fact or fiction of betrayal—then the presence of God will become treasured within our hearts. It becomes evident that we can trust God and our trust in Him gives us the ability to walk through the pain without becoming bitter. The peace of God that passes all understanding washes over us and strengthens us.

This is one of the primary differences between the Church and the world. Everyone will face betrayal, but when you apply the principles of God to that betrayal your perception is redefined. Suffering transforms into rejuvenating strength because the presence of God takes the center stage of your life. The betrayal that consumes and rips unbelievers apart to the point where their destiny is obliterated does not happen to you because of the surpassing value of knowing Christ.

2. **The word *through* is the key to all that we experience.**

If you do not go *through* the struggle, the value of God in your life and the principles of His Kingdom will not be of any benefit to you. You will continue to face the same trials again and again without ever making progress. This is the old "going around the mountain" adage. God will not test you beyond what you can handle without a way of escape. Even if you do happen to overcome betrayal, it will return because of our fallen nature. Each time you overcome betrayal by seeing it through the eyes of the Father, you will show forth the incredible power of God that takes you to your destiny.

The greatest teacher we have is Christ's example of how He dealt with the same issues we face. After handling the perception of betrayal with Judas that became factual betrayal, Christ turned to His disciples, stressing the need to look beyond the moment. He prepared them to accept the betrayal as an event that must take place in order for the purposes of God to come to fruition. He armed them with a weapon of warfare that could be used as a shield throughout the process. We have been given this same weapon: *"A new commandment I give you, that you love one another even as I have loved you..."* (John 13:34).

Do not miss the crucial timing of this Scripture. Immediately after properly defining perceived and factual betrayal, Jesus emphasizes the necessity of love. He then explains that after you view the betrayal process with the eyes of the Father and become glorified with Him, you are lifted up closer to the presence of God because you have gone *through* the process.

The potency of betrayal can cause a person to manifest love, hate, bitterness, anger, and frustration—I have experienced all of these emotions while walking through betrayal. As I began to walk completely through the process, trusting God to cause good to emerge from the rubble, a new dynamic sprang to life within me. I realized that God loved me enough to put a betrayal in my path and I trusted Him to make the betrayal ultimately manifest into love for someone else in my life.

3. **The answer to overcoming betrayal is to *love at your own expense*.**

When Jesus gave the disciples the new commandment to *love one another*, He was giving them the key that would enable them to continue moving forward in establishing the Kingdom of God. He knew that betrayal would allow the disciples to love in a greater capacity than ever before.

The answer to betrayal is not hatred, bitterness, anger, or frustration—it is love. True love is never at the expense of someone else. Again, Jesus is our example as He loves us at His expense. The Father, too, loves us at His own expense. He sent His son and gave Him out of a heart of love. In the midst of the most costly betrayal in history, Jesus revealed the answer to overcoming betrayal—love.

Too many times in society today, the word "love" is thrown around like a catch phrase, describing an emotion toward everything from the family pet to fast food. People would not be so quick to use the word if they truly realized the reaching requirements and effects of love. Real love is giving my life for someone else, not just dying for someone but forgiving someone, giving up bitterness and my humanistic response to betrayal. The general reaction of man toward betrayal is to return evil for evil and insult for insult. Someone hurts you, you fire back. The Bible says that we should not do this; instead, we are commanded to give a blessing so that we will inherit the blessing. The blessing is giving and receiving love rather than hatred, bitterness, anger, or frustration.

This is a much easier truth to write about than to live out because we must first deal with our human nature. We glamorize Jesus and tend to think that because He was God and man that it was easy for Him to love in the cruelty of betrayal. In truth, the only way for Him to speak these words of instruction concerning love to His disciples was for Him to look through the eyes of the Father in Heaven. Because He had seen the Father love people at His own expense, Jesus could then turn around and love the disciples at His expense. This should be the mark of a true believer today, according to the

Word: *"By this, all men will know you are my disciples if you have love for one another"* (John 13:35). If we will walk through the process of betrayal in love, the world will know without question that we are true disciples of Christ.

The solution seems so simple, so why doesn't the world, or the Church for that matter, see that the principles in God's Word really work? Because we must *submit constantly* to the renewing process: *"...be not conformed to this world, but be ye transformed by the renewing of your mind"* (Rom. 12:2 KJV). Through the renewing process, we prove what God's good, acceptable and perfect will is. We remove the old data that has been lodged in our mindsets and replace it with the new data we draw out of God's Word. Then, we begin to apply the information to our lives. We walk in the reality of God's love, displaying it toward others. We do not return insults or curses, we do not slander or justify ourselves—we simply love. This is how people recognize us as students of the Way, sons and daughters of God.

Writing this drives me to the reality of my own life, to the many times when I did not express the love of God because of the stubbornness of my humanity. Still, there have been times when I have put aside my will and walked in the love of God and have overcome betrayal, so it is possible for me to face it again and come through. Betrayal has been overcome thoroughly, not only because of what the Son of God has done but also because empowered men and women walk in the principles of God everyday. They have overcome betrayal by a process of loving other people at their expense, by caring for others and serving them. They have learned the reward of returning blessing for evil.

4. **To effectively overcome betrayal, we must** *see through God's eyes.*

The perception of betrayal can rise up at any time, in any relationship. We must learn how to look at every situation through the eyes of God, rather than trusting our humanity. In the last days of Christ, Peter had an idea about what would take place and it caused him to experience the perception of betrayal. Jesus would be leaving him. He would be taken away by the Jewish leadership and tortured. Later, Peter would find himself sitting in a courtyard at a fire—denying and rejecting Christ three times.

How do you leave the embrace of intimacy and end up in the seat of the scorner? Peter perceived that Jesus was not going to take him with Him. In effect, he betrayed Jesus because he felt abandoned. Although he had promised to die for Christ, he quickly rejected God and betrayed the Word of the Lord in his life. He viewed the events through the eyes of his humanity and completely missed what Jesus had done. By leaving, Jesus secured for all people a greater presence of God to be released in the earth.

As we begin to grab hold of what God is saying to us and view life through His eyes, situations take on a different light. Everyday of my life, I face various types of frustration. As mentioned previously, my wife and I travel across the United States in a motorcoach dedicating many hours of ministry to pastors and their leadership. In the course of a week, I may only preach one or two times while spending the majority of the days sowing into the lives of leadership. Yet, it is amazing to me how many times it seems that I see no fruit of our labors. When it's time to move on, we pack up the coach and head down the road, only to have it break down or to encounter another problem that may cost us thousands of dollars. This is our life on the road.

In the past, before I had an understanding of betrayal and the power of perception, I would find myself waking up asking the same question each morning, "God, I am out here doing what you want me to do and everything is going wrong. What am I doing wrong?" All of us have felt this way at least once. Whether we are struggling with an issue in our home, at our job or with our vehicle, we want to know *why* we are going through the problem. It is almost as if we are saying, "The motorcoach (household, situation at work, car, etc.) betrayed me." The fact is that the motorcoach does not have a mind of its own and it has not betrayed me. It simply stopped functioning properly.

I came to the place where I could wake up, look at the situation in my life, and deal with the reality through the eyes of God. There are issues that we all face by default of living on this planet. One of the facts of life is that we will face betrayal, perceived or factual. We have the choice to either view it through God's eyes and exalt Him, or we can deal with it through our humanity and let bitterness, anger and frustration control us and lead us away from Him.

PERCEPTION VERSUS FACT

Most betrayal enters into our lives by perception, not by fact, although both affect us. This means that the majority of the time, betrayal comes from our interpretation of an action or statement and not from someone who is intentionally attempting to harm us. Regardless of how it begins, the core issue of betrayal comes down to trusting the Father. It is about learning how to see the situation and the struggle through the eyes of God.

As a young man, I joined the Marine Corps and served in Vietnam from 1962 through 1963. Back then, the 2nd Marine Recon developed teams that trained together, ate the same food, drank the same drinks, and for all intents and purposes, did everything exactly the same. We were beyond family.

During one operation, we were attacked and all were killed except me and one other member of the team. My leg was shot and shrapnel had seared through my stomach. When I regained consciousness, my stomach was between my legs. I was a scared kid but I loved my team and I could not accept the agonizing thought of losing even one of them. I fixed myself up as best as I could and went to see if I could help anyone else. The scene was indescribable and unforgettable. In the end, the only other survivor was Bobby. I carried him on my back as far as I could until I passed out. We were later found by a chopper and lifted out of the area.

The Marine Corps has a statement, "Everybody goes home." I watched as the men removed Bobby from the chopper. As my stretcher was lifted, all I could think of were the men still lying in the field. I looked up at an officer sitting in the chopper as they were dragging me out and said, "We have to go back right now and get those men." Heartache at the thought of leaving men behind was a more severe pain than the wounds that tore through my body. I felt I was betraying my brothers because I had left them in the field and it was wrong. I would not let go of the chopper until the officer gave me his word that they would go back and get the men. Once I had that I let go physically, but I never let go inside. I was taken to a hospital and returned to the United States.

After my discharge, the Corps gave me battle ribbons but I did not see myself as a hero. I did not feel as if I had done anything brave or honorable. All I knew was that I did not do enough to keep the rest of the team alive. That betrayal became locked in the silence of my mind; I never spoke a word of my experiences. Two years ago, I was honored to go back to Camp Lejeune and minister in a church. There, God delivered me from the enemy's hand and released me from that haunting experience which I had carried for years. By suppressing the bitterness, I had cut off all of the great times—the love, camaraderie and brotherhood that I had shared with those men. God gave that back to me.

As I travel around the world, I see people everywhere reacting to the terrible things that happen in war. Yet, we must understand that the feelings of betrayal and dishonor present themselves because we do not see life long-term. I have written about Paul telling Timothy to war the war of warfare. We must occupy until Jesus comes and we must submit to the process. A significant part of going through betrayal, perceived or factual, is that you learn how to walk through with your eyes full of the handiwork of God and no matter what you are facing, you walk all the way through it.

I held on to the struggle I had as a Marine for four decades and rejected the thought of walking through it. Once God healed me, He opened my eyes to see the joy of the journey. I realized that going through trials would make God's presence in my life greater. I became a reservoir to help other people and serve their destiny. Now, I can look back at experiences that once cultivated bitterness and anger in my life and see them with a different understanding of love, loyalty and fellowship. My trust in the Father enables me to carry a new mantra—*Semper Fi*— "Forever Faithful."

Christ carried this same mantra. He loved His Father and trusted Him to the point that He could endure the betrayal of a man who had walked with him daily for over three years. This man had heard everything He had taught. He carried the money box, walked through adversity with Him, and yet when he betrayed Christ, the love of the Father in the Son of God was able to endure that treachery. If we do not see beyond the struggle, we will never make it through the process alive. We must see the other side of betrayal, whether it is perceived or factual, and we must see it through God's eyes rather than our own.

If we do not see beyond the struggle, we will never get through the process.

THERE IS NO EXPLANATION

There is a place of rest where we can take refuge after we see life through the Father's perspective. This is where we should retreat to at the end of the day, because sometimes there is no explanation for why certain things happen. When you walk through betrayal of any kind, it is easy to become hung up on trying to rationalize the perfect answer to an imperfect problem. The truth is that we do not have to have the answer to every problem we face. We do not have to make a judgment when people do things and we do not have to conjure up something to minister to them. We have all walked through issues and tried to find the best way to correct the situation. Sometimes walking through betrayal does not have anything to do with other people.

Jesus never did anything to correct the problem with the one who betrayed Him. When Jesus began to predict Judas' betrayal, He did not take Judas to the side to correct the problem or try to find a way to minister truth to him. Jesus did not proclaim a judgment against him or degrade him. Jesus loved.

Love is the same answer for us today. Scripture tells us to rejoice with those who rejoice and weep with those who weep. Realize that there will be times when you are ministering to people who are going through the devastation of betrayal—you do not have to bring the answer to them, you do not have to correct them or adjust their lives. All they need to know is that you weep with them, you rejoice with them and you love them.

As believers, we have to go to the next level. When Jesus made the statement that, *"...the Son of man is glorified..."* He was telling the world that He would be taking the Church to another place of glory. There is a new dimension in God where the Father's love can be expressed to the world in a way that has never been comprehended. This is a clear promise in Scripture:

> *But a natural man does not accept the things of the Spirit of God; for they are foolishness to him, and he cannot understand them, because they are spiritually appraised. But he who is spiritual appraises all things, yet he himself is appraised by no man. For **who has known the mind of the Lord, that he should instruct him?** But we have the mind of Christ* (1 Corinthians 2:14-16, emphasis added).

When an individual walks through betrayal or sees someone else walking through betrayal, the situation must be spiritually discerned. We cannot continue to look at betrayal through the eyes of flesh and expect to come up with the right answer. Our efforts to bring answers or explanations to someone who is in the process will be totally unproductive. A wrong suffered is a wrong suffered and that cannot be changed. True freedom from the pain of betrayal is realized only when others become equipped to shift their view from the short-term to the long-term and see the example of our lives as we walk through the trial without bitterness. When we let others spiritually appraise what God has done and is doing in our lives, they will become empowered to overcome the betrayal in their lives. This is how we share the love of God and glorify His Son.

HEALING FROM BETRAYAL

Openly sharing the love of God and exposing yourself to His healing touch is the only way to fully recover from betrayal. If you try to build a wall and then attempt to hide behind that wall, you are only deceiving yourself. Others will always see the wall that guards you, the bitterness that enslaves you, or the open wounds that vex. They see them more clearly than you, because you have grown accustomed to them. Sometimes you just need someone to grab hold of your feet and lift you up so that you can see the true state of yourself. That is not to imply that you always need someone to give you an answer. Still, others who have successfully walked through the pain of betrayal can help by sharing the love of God with you.

Until you are healed from the bitterness in your heart caused by betrayal, you will never be able to love someone else through it—to help them find the difference between truth and perception of truth. You have to let the hurt go completely, walk through the process, and let the Lord take you into a love relationship with Him. You must come to the place where you can see that betrayal is not the end of your life or the lives of others.

Chapter 12

IT IS FINISHED

I love you. These three powerful words can sometimes seem hollow when you hear them in the midst of the heartache of betrayal. This is why counseling, therapy, and even good advice from friends will never fully heal you from the devastating effects of betrayal. There is only one Man who has gone through the depths of blackest betrayal and finished the course. Jesus did so much more than secure our salvation through His death and resurrection.

Remember when Jesus gave the keys of the Kingdom to Peter, unlocking his destiny (see Matthew 16:19)? Today, those keys belong to every believer in order to unlock the destiny and purposes of God for your generation and generations that follow. In order to wield these keys effectively, believers must first fully understand the complete picture of what happened, naturally and spiritually, behind the scenes leading up to the last of days of Christ.

LIFE OR DEATH

The truth of all that has been written in this book is based on betrayal being part of our fallen nature. It started in the heavenlies, was repeated in the Garden and has been fostered throughout the ages by satan as well as humankind. Sin is a result of the betrayal of God's creation against God Himself. When Christ came and fulfilled His purpose, the stronghold of betrayal was defeated. The fuse of self-promotion and pride that had been lit by the enemy's mutiny, causing flames of bitterness and accusation throughout history, was vanquished by the obedience of Jesus and His overwhelming love for the Father.

In one of the most critical moments in history, the Word of God proved that *"...Love never fails..."* (see 1 Cor. 13). Love overcomes, or annihilates, betrayal. All of the failures of man are covered by love.

"It is finished" (John 19:30)

With His final breath, Jesus proclaimed these words. Now, it is no longer an issue of thinking that our failures will be covered by love, that rejection can be replaced with approval, or that betrayal could be overcome. Our failures are covered by love, we are able to draw approval from the Father, and betrayal has been overcome because of Jesus' unwavering love and obedience

Many theologians and scholars have theorized that Jesus' last statement was referring to His sacrifice made to cover the sin of man. That idea has been so glorified that it has overshadowed the intensity of what I believe actually took place. The blood of the unstained Lamb spilled onto the earth and soaked the ground beneath the Cross; His earthly life was waning. Beneath the surface, Light and darkness were locked in the balance. In seconds, the veil between God and man would be rent from top to bottom. But first, a long-standing offense would be settled forever.

FORSAKEN YET BELOVED

Now from the sixth hour darkness fell upon the land until the ninth hour. About the ninth hour Jesus cried out with a loud voice, saying, **"Eli, eli, lama sabachthani?"** *that is,* **"My God, my God, why have you forsaken me?"** (Matthew 27:45-46, emphasis added)

During the 33 years Jesus walked on the earth, He recognized God as His Father. He had continually sought out the Father's heart and walked accordingly. His entire life had been spent forsaking His own will and carrying out the will of the Father. Now, at the end of His life, instead of being received before Heaven and embraced by the Father, He is scorned by all of humanity and the Father Himself. This is the only time that Jesus uses the term, "My God." The Father turned His head because He could not look at the sin of the world shrouding His Son. Whether this happened in fact or whether it was perception, the result is the same: Jesus is forsaken by the Father and the abandonment is beyond human comprehension. He felt that His intimacy with the Father had been stripped from Him.

When God the Father turned His back, the humanity of Christ cried out with great distress and suffering; yet, He understood His purpose and was confident in His identity. He knew more than anyone the ravages of betrayal and that no man would ever be able to bridge the rift caused by this destructive tool prized by satan. Jesus trusted the Father; even though He asked why He was being forsaken, He knew that His obedience would lead to humanity's freedom and turn the tide on betrayal. His question was a result of the struggle between His spirit and humanity as the agonizing grief ripped through Him. Ultimately, He released His own will and embraced the will of the Father.

All men go through struggles and use the same words that Jesus cried out while on the Cross. We face trials and hardships and start to question God about where His presence is in our lives. We ask, "Why am I going through this? What have I done? Why has God turned away from me when I have done just what He asked me to do?" Our human nature looks for an explanation of why betrayal comes rather than seeing the glory that will result from our obedience as we stay true to the course.

As long as satan is the prince and the power of the air and we live in this human body, he has power to deceive, lie and condemn. This is his nature. He uses these tactics to try and get us to the point where we will betray the Father. When we find ourselves in a place where God is not in our midst and it seems that betrayal is consuming us, we feel as if God has forsaken us. We find ourselves asking, "Father, where are you? Why am I alone?" The further we dive into indulging our calamities, the more we begin to question and then accuse. This is when, if we lose sight of purpose, we end up becoming the betrayer.

Luke 23:39 gives the account of the two criminals who hung on either side of Jesus. They had been proven guilty and were paying penance for their crimes. One of the criminals, eaten up with rage and frustration, hurled abuses at Jesus. He spitefully asked, *"Are you not the Christ? Save yourself and save me."* In a terrible wrenching time of distress, he was questioning everything, hurling abuses and falling into the depths of being forsaken (see Luke 23:39).

The second criminal offered an opposite reaction. He rebukes the first and asks him, *"Do you not even fear God?"* (see Luke 23:40-43). He is not referring to a fear of torment; he is talking about having an understanding of God—having the fear of the Lord that is the beginning of wisdom. This criminal knew that he was rightly charged for crimes he had committed and that he was deserving of punishment. His knowledge of Jesus as the Christ made him defend, rather than accuse, Jesus.

The second criminal knew that Jesus was innocent, and his understanding allowed him to see beyond the current situation and press into the Lord. By recognizing that he had pursued his own selfish will above a relationship with the Lord, he was able to come to the end of himself and asked to be changed: *"...Jesus, Lord, remember me when You come into Your kingdom..."* (Luke 23:42 NKJV). This man was actually saying, "God I want to trust you. Even though I have violated and disobeyed You by trusting in myself, even though I have betrayed You, please remember me."

What would you have said? What have you said to others who have come back to ask forgiveness for trespasses against you? Our natural response is to say that the criminal was guilty and deserving of hell. Jesus responded with mercy and grace: *"...today, you will be with Me in paradise..."* (Luke 23:43). Jesus embraced His destiny as the Restorer of our right relationship with God to the very end. He continued to pour out the Father's love to others even in the midst of being forsaken by the Father because His identity had been borne out of intimacy that had manifested into unshakable trust.

Betrayal always reveals who you trust. Whenever it looks as if someone has turned away from us or forsaken us, our human nature causes us to draw back and erect a shield of defense. We stop loving at our own expense and become more concerned with self-preservation, but Jesus was focused on a greater cause than His human life. When Jesus would not supernaturally prove Himself as King by coming down from the Cross, carnal and even spiritually religious men began to mock Him saying, *"He saved others; He cannot save Himself? Let this Christ, the King of Israel, now come down from the cross so that we may see and believe..."* (Mark 15:31-32).

This is the cross-roads of betrayal: save yourself, your flesh and emotions or go through the process and overcome. At this point, your flesh is screaming and the victory flag seems so distant that it is barely a speck on the horizon. Jesus sensed the Father forsaking Him, the rulers were mocking him, the people were jeering, crying, and wailing. All He had to do was betray God—who, it seemed, had already turned away—and He could save Himself.

What is really being challenged here? Identity. The leaders were clamoring for Jesus to betray the very reason He had gone to the Cross. They were challenging Him with jeers about how He had saved and healed others, yet He could not save Himself. They wanted to see Jesus prove Himself through some type of divine miracle. The scribes and Pharisees were saying that if Jesus would just succumb to the Adamic nature and betray the Father, He would have a position with the people. This is the same strike at identity that satan made in the wilderness while tempting Jesus: *"...if You are the Son of God, command these stones to become bread..."* (Matt. 4:3-10). Satan had taunted Jesus to betray the Father and the things of God in return for the promise of power and position. At the base of the Cross, carnal men yelled out that same message.

If Jesus had listened to man and come off of the Cross, saying that the Father forsaking Him justified His actions, it would have nullified the love of the Son for the Father—and humanity. Yes, the Father did forsake Jesus; yet, because of intimacy, Jesus had fallen in love with the Father's heart and refused to betray that relationship by pulling Himself from the Cross. Jesus trusted the Father so much that He could see beyond His current suffering, beyond the mocking and the pain of humanity. Jesus saw the Kingdom of God, and He saw the kingdom of darkness overcome by the love of God.

Jesus stayed focused on the Father and His plan for all people. His actions set in place the platform for a spiritual kingdom far beyond our comprehension. This was a kingdom birthed in the heavens that would be made manifest on the earth. Jesus looked so far beyond the moment that He saw the Kingdom of God descending from on high to the earth and capturing a people who betrayed Him. When Jesus declared the words of Isaiah, *"The spirit of the Lord is upon me, because he anointed me to preach the Gospel to the poor, He has sent me to proclaim release to the captives, and recovery of sight to the blind, to set free those who are oppressed"* (Luke 4:18), He was talking about setting the captive free from the works of betrayal. Christ secured a freedom that releases us from our sinful nature. He destroyed the place satan used to burn accusation or deception into our lives in an effort to stop us from bringing forth the love of God upon the earth.

BREAKING THE CURSE

Jesus overturned every tactic the enemy had used to detour God's creation in the past. In the midst of ridicule, torture, and accusation, Jesus said, *"...Father, forgive them; for they do not know what they are doing..."* (Luke 23:34). He had a clear and precise understanding of the death process. His sacrifice was not just to bury sin; it was to break the curse that had been placed on us through the original sin.

I have written in detail about the sins of the father going unto the third and fourth generation in the book, *Spiritual Mentor*. The curse of a father travels down a family line through the ages, but in one request for forgiveness Jesus broke the curse forever. In His appeal to the Father, He offered up Himself so we could be freed. Jesus stood in the gap to break the generational curse caused by the devil, by the works of betrayal.

Anytime we reject the truth in order to pursue our own will, we are following after the nature of satan. When Jesus had originally revealed that He would die, Peter rebuked Him. Jesus responded that Peter was of his father, the devil, because he was perpetuating the curse that had fallen upon all creation through the sin that occurred in the Garden. God had revealed to Peter that Jesus was the Christ, the Son of the Living God. Now Peter was fostering betrayal toward that revelation because he was after his own will—the will of the devil. The crowd at the base of the Cross did not understand that in chanting for Jesus' death, they were actually securing a platform for the breaking of the curse upon humanity.

Three powerful words broke the curse and reconciled man to God, *"...Father, forgive them..."* (Luke 23:34).

IT IS FINISHED

And behold, the veil of the temple was torn in two from the top to the bottom, and the earth shook; and the rocks were split. The tombs opened; and many bodies of the saints who had fallen asleep were raised and coming out of the tombs after His resurrection they entered the holy city and appeared to many. Now the centurion, and those who were with him keeping guard over Jesus, when they saw the earthquake

*and the things that were happening, became very frightened and said,
"Truly this was the Son of God!"* (Matthew 27:51-54).

Betrayal was subdued by the hand of God and truth became
evident to every person alive; even the earth itself cried out.
The privilege to commune with and relate to God has been
restored to all, forever. There is one moment that must be
reflected on to ensure a full understanding of the freedom and
healing that you have been made a recipient of through God's
unwavering love.

THE TASTE OF BETRAYAL AND THE TOUCH OF REJECTION

Once Jesus had set matters in order for His mother to now relate to John the Beloved, He said that He was thirsty. At the cru-
cifixion site, there was a basin of sour wine made from spoiled or
bitter grapes. Some say it may have been bitter vinegar. In either
case, the cup of guile contained a very toxic liquid that was not
intended to quench thirst, but to increase agony.

A hyssop branch was dipped into the cup and then placed
onto Jesus' lips. This type of branch was used to separate life
and death for the Israelites. In the past, it had been used to dip
into the blood of the lamb and spread that blood over the
doorpost so that the spirit of death could not enter. On this
day, the hyssop branch soaked in the liquid of bitterness
touched the lips of Jesus, but it did not touch His heart. The
Word of God says that, *"...Jesus [...] received the sour wine..."* (John
19:30). This simply means that the branch brought the wine of
bitterness to Jesus' lips but He did not take it in or drink of it.
Jesus tasted betrayal when the Father turned His back, but it
did not consume His heart.

The bitter liquid offered to Jesus was a symbol of the Father
turning away. Jesus could have drunk the bitterness, but He did

not. He could have perceived that the Father had betrayed Him, but He would not. His love so overwhelmed His natural man that He was able to say "Betrayal is finished." Jesus reunited the Father with His creation through the cry of His own intimacy and agony. Even though the Father would not look upon Him, His love for the Father was so strong that betrayal could not penetrate it. Betrayal was given no place in His life. The work of the destroyer was destroyed.

The phrase "it is finished" is not just a conclusion to all that Jesus had done or accomplished. It is not only referring to the fulfillment of prophetic words. These three words make up the seal of love that defeated the betrayal that began between satan and God, the betrayal that took place in the Garden and all betrayal affecting humanity throughout the ages. Jesus was touched with the searing fire of betrayal but He did not partake of it. His faith in the Father was so great that He knew without a doubt that the heavens would open. He would be received back into the arms of His Holy Father. Christ had fulfilled the destiny and purpose the Father had placed on His life. Then, Jesus gave up His spirit.

How Important Are You?

That is not the end of the story and it is not the end of satan's attempts to use betrayal against our fallen nature. Scripture shows us the reactions of the disciples after Jesus is buried. They are lost and empty. This band of believers, who had witnessed unsurpassed miracles and powerful acts, now hid away in Jerusalem in fear of the scribes and Pharisees. Peter is completely undone and torn apart with rejection. Mary is sobbing at the tomb early in the darkness of morning. She cannot comprehend why the tomb is empty. Running away, she describes the scene at the tomb to the disciples. James and John run ahead of

Peter to the tomb and cannot find anything. Peter looks around without finding Jesus. Now, even the body of Christ is missing! They were utterly confused.

I cannot articulate the urgency behind the people of God coming to a revelation and an understanding of betrayal. We are just as confused today as this group who searched for Christ's body. Betrayal has infected the Church and the world by weaving a nasty thread throughout all circumstances. Brother rises up against brother, daughter against mother, minister against minister, and friend against friend. The arrows of betrayal pierce our very souls and we search earnestly for Christ, while feeling shaken and alone.

Ask yourself, "How important am I?" How important are you in the lonely times of life when you feel as if you have been betrayed and everything and everyone has forsaken you? You may have even felt that God Himself has turned His back on you. Remember this: Jesus came forth from the tomb and has secured your freedom!

The Bible teaches in Ephesians that He ascended, but before that, He first descended and led a host of captives. On His way back up to the Father, He stopped by the tomb where Mary was sobbing uncontrollably. She was perplexed and frightened, vacant of heart. Mary was probably the loneliest person on the face of the earth at that time. She looked up to see a man whom she perceived to be a gardener and pleaded with him to reveal the location of the body. Then she heard the Voice.

If you will shift your focus from the betrayal and the process of walking through betrayal and look beyond the moment, you will behold the glory of God. Jesus, the Son of the Living God, will reveal Himself. You are so important to Christ that He stopped in the middle of His ascension to the Father and to His rightful throne to let us know that He is alive. Just as He comforted Mary and told her to find Peter and give him the news of His resurrection, He will single you out and strengthen you with hope.

Jesus gave specific instructions for Mary to find Peter because He had told Peter that satan desired to sift him. Then Jesus reassured Peter that He would pray for him, and He charged him to remember to strengthen the brethren once he overcame the sifting of the enemy. Jesus knew that as soon as Peter heard Mary's report, he would begin to strengthen the brethren with the fact that Jesus had not betrayed them. Peter would reassure the others that the Kingdom would be established just as Jesus had said. For 40 days, Jesus appeared to the disciples after His resurrection, dealing with them and bringing healing, strength and courage. He confronted Thomas' doubt. Though Thomas was ashamed, he was never forsaken, just as Peter was never forsaken and we will never be forsaken.

The answer to betrayal is love. Jesus has expressed His love to me time and time again through spoken love, revealed love and touched love. He loves you with that same intensity. There is a prayer that I have prayed over the years that has become more and more alive to me as time goes on. Please say this prayer together with me and our proclamation will affect change upon the earth, upon our lives and upon the sons and daughters of God:

> I proclaim in the heavenlies, I announce on the earth, betrayal will no longer have control over my life. I choose not to foster betrayal nor let it come into my life and rule me. Father, I make a choice to love as Your Son has loved. I make a choice to reveal to the world that the betrayal in the Adamic nature of man no longer has a hold on me. Not only has the curse been broken on

the earth, that curse is broken in my life. Now, Father, I bring the blessing upon the sons and daughters, upon the creation of God, upon that which You have spoken upon the earth.

Father, let it be upon me and upon Your children.

In Jesus name I pray, Amen.

Ministry Contact Information

To contact Ron DePriest or to obtain additional copies of this book and other resources provided through this ministry please write to:

World Impact Network
5 Edgebrook Court
Cleburne, TX 76033

Or reach us on the Internet at:

WWW.rondepriest.com

More Resources
by Ron DePriest

A contract on his life couldn't stop Ron DePriest from preaching the Gospel of Jesus Christ.

This true story reads like a high-action novel beyond the imagination of any movie director. A murderer on an inescapable mission from God follows a pattern he cannot prevent with a destiny God will not deny. Dozens of attempts on his life span three decades of road trip missions as a "successful Christian." Then he decides to take his own life.

"Loco! My closest friends called me by my patch name. How crazy do you have to be for crazy people to call you crazy? I often wondered why I was still alive.-after childhood beatings, motorcycle accidents, gun fights, knife fights, my entire squad wiped out in war, prison, every major bone broken at least once...but through it all, I survived. Why?"

This book gives hope and purpose to everyone who has ever asked—Why am I alive? Ron DePriest's shocking story touches the heart's hidden depths to clarify life's essential questions and illustrates God's willingness to fix what people ruin.

A Death He Couldn't Stop
A Life He Couldn't Live

With God All Things Are Possible

A testimonial DVD in which Ron shares his life story which coordinates with his book, *Loco*. This is also available as a CD.

Other products are available from Ron DePriest by contacting us through the Website: www.rondepriest.com.

World Impact Partners

For a number of years we have worked to serve and impact people. We believe God has given us an avenue to serve that purpose with Impact Partners. As you know we have ministered for over three decades. The mandate given to us from God is to sow into the lives and destiny of men and women around the world. Our main call is to invest ourselves into the vision and destiny of God's people. What this means is simply that you would make a commitment for a year of $25 per month and for this you will receive a CD each month. This CD will be recorded only for you, the Impact Partners and not for the resource table. Also for this yearly commitment you will receive a letter from Minnie each month keeping you informed of all that is happening, where we are heading next and things about the family. Also, if you have prayer needs please send us a note with your seed faith money and it shall be prayed for.

Name: _____

Address: _____

City: _____ State: _____ Zip: _____

Phone Number: _____

E-mail: _____

PAYMENT OPTIONS :

Checks: _____

Credit cards via the Internet (Pay Pal): _____

Money order: _____

PLEASE MAIL TO:

World Impact Network
6528 Merwin Ave.
Cincinnati, OH 45227